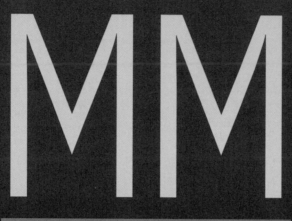

Understanding and Composing Multimodal Projects

MM Understanding and Composing Multimodal Projects

≡ MM1 Introduction

In many of your college courses, you will be asked to read, analyze, and compose texts. The way you interact with texts can determine your success in college. The good news is that you have been reading, analyzing, and composing for years. Think of a magazine you read often, a job ad you once replied to, a Web site you've frequently visited, a book you discussed with friends, or a Facebook comment you recently made. Your college courses may give you the opportunity to analyze and compose *multimodal* texts as well, texts that rely on a combination of modes, such as images, words, and sounds, to communicate an idea. A common example is a print advertisement, a text that communicates meaning with both words and an image.

Understanding and Composing Multimodal Projects will help you take a broader look at yourself as a reader and as a writer.

MM1-a What does it mean to "read" a text?

This book asks you to take a new look at the act of reading. You know that a person can read an article, but can he "read" a painting? Someone can read a book, of course, but can she "read" a podcast? Your immediate answer might be "No, of course not!" but if you can rethink what it means to read—and consider that reading can mean taking a closer look or listening critically—your answer might be "Well, maybe!" This book also asks you to reconsider what is meant by the word text. Most people would call an essay or a poem a text. Can a movie soundtrack or a cartoon be called a text?

To dig into these terms, compare John Keats's drawing in Figure 1–1 (p. MM-6), an ancient urn, with his 1819 poem "Ode on a Grecian Urn." What are the characteristics that might lead us to call the drawing a text? What are the characteristics that might lead us to call the poem a text? How would we "read" the image of the urn? How do we "read" the poem?

Here is an excerpt from Keats's "Ode on a Grecian Urn":

> O Attic shape! Fair attitude! with brede
> Of marble men and maidens overwrought,
> With forest branches and the trodden weed;
> Thou, silent form, dost tease us out of thought
> As doth eternity: Cold Pastoral!
> When old age shall this generation waste,
> Thou shalt remain, in midst of other woe
> Than ours, a friend to man, to whom thou say'st,
> "Beauty is truth, truth beauty,"—that is all
> Ye know on earth, and all ye need to know.

If reading means discovering what a text is saying, it's helpful to consider how the text is presenting its meaning. In the poem, meaning is presented through written words. The drawing shows details from the actual urn, including images that communicate meaning. Both "texts" tell a story for a purpose and to an audience.

Reading may also require careful attention to the historical and cultural context in which a text is created. A text always emerges out of a time and a place and a social situation. To read Keats's poem effectively may require knowing something about the English Romantic literary movement. To read the image of the urn effectively may require a familiarity with the uses of urns and other pottery in ancient Greece.

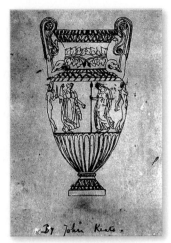

FIGURE 1–1 JOHN KEATS'S DRAWING OF AN ANCIENT URN.

Almost anything can be read—that is, carefully approached and analyzed for *what* it does and *how* it does what it does. Almost anything can be a text—that is, something that conveys meaning. Reading carefully and critically often means asking questions about a text. When and by whom was the text created? What purpose was it intended to serve? What assumptions does the creator or composer make about the audience? Reading for a college course requires active, thoughtful investigation.

MM1-b What is multimodal composing?

This book refers to texts that include more than one way of presenting an idea as *multimodal*. Multimodal texts are those that draw on multiple (multi) modes of conveying information, including words, numbers, images, graphics, animations, transitions, sounds (voice and music), and more.

WORDS   = MONOMODAL TEXT

WORDS + [_____]   = MULTIMODAL TEXT

When ancient orators, or public speakers, tried to persuade audiences, they did so orally with the words they spoke and their tone of voice—but they also did so with another mode, their physical gestures.

Speakers throughout history have communicated their meaning by combining modes, or ways of presenting their message. The best, most convincing speakers know that a gesture combined with a word can be powerful—and when the word is spoken in a particular tone, it can be even more so. Clasped, raised hands can convey pleading or imploring, for instance, while a clenched fist often conveys might and strength.

SPEECH + GESTURES = MULTIMODAL TEXT

This is multimodal composing.

Think back to a high school earth science class, where you may have been studying earthquakes and plate tectonics. You may have had to compose a project that called for diagrams to represent the different types of plate movements within the earth's crust; a report on the specific physical features of a recent earthquake—Indonesia (2007), Chile (2010), Haiti (2010), or Japan (2011); and a brief slide show presentation of cause-and-effect findings to the class.

WORDS + IMAGES + SPEECH = MULTIMODAL TEXT

This is multimodal composing.

Using multiple modes causes us to rethink terminology. You may be accustomed to referring to those who compose texts as *authors* or *writers*. You may also use the term *writing* to describe most acts of communicating ideas. This book will describe communicating ideas as *composing*, which literally means "to produce something by putting together." And this book will refer to those who compose multimodal texts as *composers*.

Composers of texts may combine modes, and in some ways this makes their work more complicated. Composers have more options for sending a message, sharing an idea, posing an argument, teaching other people how to do something, and so forth. In other ways, combining modes makes composers' work more exciting and effective. They can send, share, teach, and explain in ways that include words *and* other elements.

MM1-c Composing *hasn't* changed

In some ways, composing has not changed all that much. It has always been crucial to how meaning is made and shared—how we communicate ideas from person to person, community to community, and generation to generation. Composing has always served to capture, save, and deliver ideas, messages, and meanings. Ancient cultures, for example, composed petroglyphs, rock carvings on cave walls and the sides of mountains, to share their ideas in a lasting way (Figure 1–2).

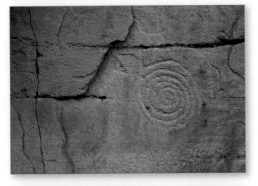

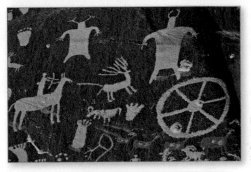

FIGURE 1–2 ANCIENT PETROGLYPHS ON CAVE WALLS.

(*Source:* US National Park Service; Pgiam)

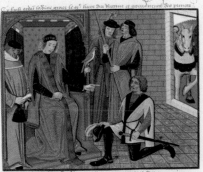

FIGURE 1–3 MEDIEVAL ILLUMINATED MANUSCRIPT.

(*Source:* Duncan Walker)

Further, composing has often, to some extent, been multimodal. As far back as the fifth century CE, for example, monks created illuminated manuscripts—richly decorated books that combined illustrations and words. (Figure 1–3).

Though today's printed brochures aren't handwritten or decorated with gold leaf, they are a similarly effective combination of modes (words and images). Think about a catalog that includes full-color, glossy pages and perhaps a QR (quick response) code you can scan with your cell phone for more information (Figure 1–4). Or think about an e-book, which might include the typical contents of a printed book—a table of contents, numbered pages, lots of text, and so on—but which can also contain embedded video clips and animations.

FIGURE 1–4 QR (QUICK RESPONSE) CODE. (*Source:* Denso Wave Incorporated)

MM1-d Composing *has* changed

Composing has, in some ways, changed significantly in recent years. Today's composers blog, podcast, craft digital stories, prepare slide show presentations, design Web pages, write short blurbs to post as status updates and news, and much more. The ways in which composing has changed result primarily from a few recent technological innovations:

- The speed with which we can share and distribute documents. No longer do we have to take the time to print a document and mail it to others; instead, we can zip it along to others via e-mail or social media spaces.

- The ease with which we can draw on multiple media in one document. Word processing applications, for instance, allow writers to incorporate images. Web page creation spaces encourage composers to embed links to video-sharing sites like YouTube.

- Access to a range of media and materials. When writers wanted to compose a multimodal document before computer software made it easy to do so, they would have to physically cut and paste—with scissors and glue—to embed images in a textual document. Today, electronic copy-and-paste functions allow writers to almost seamlessly pull media from different online spaces and move those media across applications.

Together, these changes provide a broader context for composing *and* for sharing texts. Both the composers of centuries-old

manuscripts and the composers of days-old YouTube videos thought about their purposes for communicating, the audiences they were trying to reach, the technology available to them at the time, and which modes were most useful in communicating their ideas.

MM1-e Composing in college

Most academic work involves producing traditional written pages that demonstrate certain elements of good writing: attention to your purpose and your audience; clear thesis statements; strong, well-formed paragraphs; evidence that might include citations and examples; bibliographies or works cited pages; and so on. Across academic disciplines, you'll be expected to approach, understand, and analyze different types of multimodal texts as well.

1. $-5y + 3 = 2(4y + 12)$

2. $\frac{4}{x^2 - 2x} - \frac{2}{x - 2} = -\frac{1}{2}$

3. $x\sqrt{x} = -x$

4. $|x - a| = a^2 - x^2$

5. $4x^2 + 1 - 2x^2 + 2 = 8$

6. $\log_2(2x - 1) + x = \log_4(144)$

7. $\begin{cases} x^2 + y^2 = 17 + 2x \\ (x - 1)^2 + (y - 8)^2 = 34 \end{cases}$

FIGURE 1–5 A MULTI-MODAL TEXT FROM A MATH COURSE.
(*Source:* umsolver.com)

For instance, in math courses, you will encounter equations that include not only numbers but also a range of shapes and figures with particular meaning (Figure 1–5). In a geology or physics course, you might study images that show various movements of the earth's crust (Figure 1–6). In an art history course, you might encounter collages by famous artists and be expected to interrogate them, analyze their meaning, and talk about your response to them (Figure 1–7).

In a variety of college courses, you'll also be expected to plan, outline, and create different types of multimodal texts.

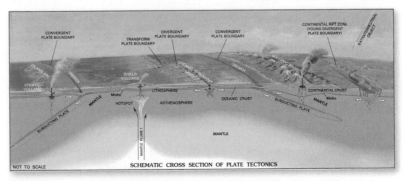

FIGURE 1–6 A MULTIMODAL TEXT FROM A GEOLOGY COURSE. (*Source:* US Geological Survey)

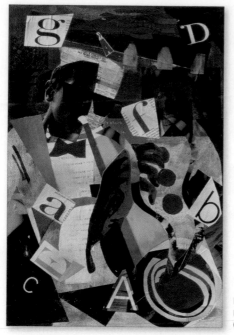

FIGURE 1–7 A MULTIMODAL TEXT FROM AN ART HISTORY COURSE. (*Source:* Gilbert Mayer)

In an introduction to economics course, you might be asked to work in a group to prepare and present a slide show analyzing financial trends.

For an English class, you might be asked to write weekly blog posts in response to assigned readings.

In a biology class, you might be assigned to photograph a particular area over time to construct a visual record of the changes in foliage.

Constructing each of these multimodal texts—a slide show, a blog, a visual record—will require you to think critically and carefully about the different elements you might include (sound, video, charts, photographs, data, words) and how to compose with audience, purpose, organization, clarity, and responsibility in mind.

MM1-f Composing beyond college

College isn't the only place where you might have to analyze and produce multimodal texts. You may, for example, encounter public service ads like the one in Figure 1–8, which combines words and an image

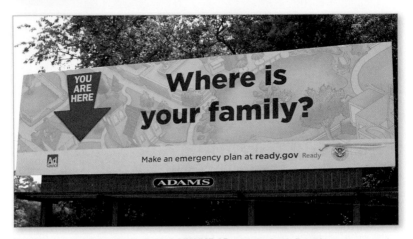

FIGURE 1-8 A MULTIMODAL PUBLIC SERVICE AD. (*Source:* Sonda Dawes)

to prompt you to think about making an emergency plan for yourself and your family. Or you may be part of a community group hosting a fundraising event, for which you'll have to create eye-catching, compelling flyers to attract both sponsors and participants.

Knowing how to produce multimodal texts will be an asset as you start to look for a job. In a 2009 document called "Workplace Writing Skills," educator Christine Polk pointed out that although businesses and organizations rely on efficient and effective communication to profit and thrive, many people struggle to write effectively in the workplace. Job ads—seeking everything from engineering architects to park rangers to grocery store managers—often emphasize the ways in which companies and organizations value candidates who can effectively communicate in multimodal ways. Job candidates today may be expected to produce projects like these:

technical reports that include data or diagrams

planning documents that communicate the rationale for and placement of products in a retail environment

announcements to the public that include text and maps or illustrations

training videos for customers or new employees

Web site content to draw in clients or customers

Analyzing and composing multimodal texts in college can give you the practice you need to communicate effectively in civic, personal, or professional situations in the future.

MM1-g What this book offers

This book is anchored by the concepts discussed in the previous sections: that is, how composing has and hasn't changed, an expanded notion of what composing is, and the importance of composing in and outside of the classroom.

This book offers the following:

a process for analyzing multimodal texts

a vocabulary for analyzing multimodal texts

a process for producing multimodal texts

a close look at two students' multimodal composing processes

a way of thinking about the relation between analyzing and producing multimodal texts

Sections MM1 through MM6 will help you hone your skills of analysis as you explore different types of modes and texts. Sections MM7 through MM15 will help you think about the best processes, practices, and tools for conveying your own ideas in a multimodal composition.

Keep in mind that effective compositions transcend specific software programs and digital spaces. If you can adopt the habits of carefully analyzing and crafting different types of texts, you will become a flexible, smart communicator who knows how to select the best tool for the job and the best techniques for the composing task at hand.

MM1-h A toolkit for analyzing and composing multimodal texts

As a first step in looking at multimodal texts, you need to learn to identify the different modes a composer is using and to examine them separately. Sections MM2 through MM6 ask you to read and analyze written words, sounds, static images, moving images, and multimodal texts. The book includes a toolkit that helps you evaluate individual modes and multimodal compositions. You will learn to think in terms of What? How? Who? and Why? as you answer questions like these in sections MM2 through MM6:

Genre. What kind of text is it? A slide show? An audio essay? An advertisement?

Features. How would you describe the elements of the text? What styles and treatments has the composer used to create emphasis, maintain clarity, or inspire feeling?

Purpose and audience. What is the text doing? For what reason was the text created? Who is the intended reader/viewer/listener?

Meaning. What is your interpretation of the text? (Keep in mind that your interpretation—your take on the meaning—may differ from the composer's intended message.)

Sections MM2 through MM6 include specific advice about how to apply these tools to different types of texts—those composed of written words, sounds, static (or still) images, or moving images—and to compositions that combine these modes.

MM2 Analyzing written words

When written words appear alone in a document, it's clear that they have a message to convey. In much academic writing, the design of the document seems "invisible," whether the message is simple or complex. In other words, academic writers often avoid decorative or unusual fonts (such as Comic Sans) or font treatments (such as color)

Analyzing written words

Genre

In what kind of document do the words appear? A brochure? A letter? An essay?

Features

Is the text in a single font or a variety of fonts? How would you describe the font(s)? Are there different colors and sizes? Do you notice bold, italic, or highlighted words? Are any words animated—do they move or change in shape, color, or size?

Purpose and audience

What is the purpose of the text? Is it meant to teach, guide, warn, entertain, or provoke the reader?

Who is the intended audience for the written words? Readers who will take time to read them? Or readers who will need to grasp the message quickly? Are they consumers, children, workers, fans, protesters, commuters, or a mixed group?

Meaning

How do genre, features, purpose, and audience work together to convey a message? How do you interpret the use of the written words? (Keep in mind that your interpretation—your take on the meaning—may differ from the composer's intended message.)

that might distract readers or discourage them from taking the message seriously.

When used thoughtfully, however, different fonts and features can add meaning to written words and can be especially appropriate in multimodal compositions. Whether created for academic, professional, or creative purposes, multimodal compositions may use a variety of treatments and even animations to boost or otherwise alter the meaning of written words. When you're analyzing how written words function in a composition, consider the questions in the chart on page MM-14.

MM2-a Genre: In what kind of document do the written words appear?

Often you'll form ideas about the content of a document as soon as you look at it, before you read a single word. Determining what type of document you're dealing with is a key step in analyzing the words within the document.

Take a look at the document thumbnails in Figure 2–1. Although you can't read all of the words, thinking about where the words appear and how the overall document is formatted will give you a sense of what kind of information the words might convey.

Look closely at image (a) on page MM-16. How much space appears between the lines of text? What do you think is the function of the words in the upper left corner? What likely appears centered after those words? Answers to these questions tell us that these words are probably part of a traditional essay, with space devoted to the author's name, course, and date in the top left and the title centered on the line below.

Now consider image (d). How are the words arranged? The way the words are chunked together and placed in columns reveals at a glance that they are words in a menu. The arrangement of words in the document tells us what kind of information to expect—a list of foods organized by course: appetizers, entrees, and desserts. Imagine trying to read a menu without categories or labels, in which all the content is lumped together without being organized or easily identifiable.

MM2-b Features: What do the words look like?

We're so used to gathering meaning from written words simply by reading them that it may seem strange at first to analyze what the words look like. Words can, however, appear in a variety of sizes, shapes, colors, styles, and static or animated configurations. One of the first things

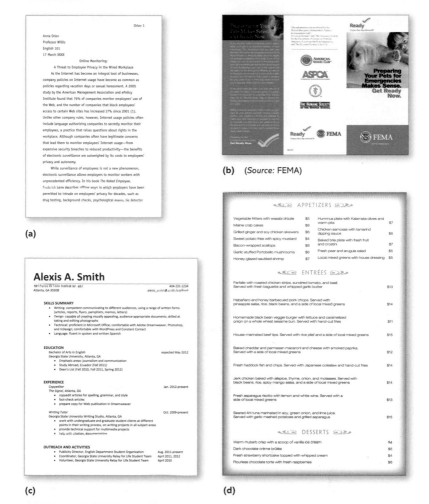

FIGURE 2-1 EVERYDAY TEXTS.

to note is the font (or *typeface*) in which the words appear. Graphic designers often talk about fonts as the "voice" of the page.

When considering the effect that font choice has on a text, think about what adjectives you might associate with a particular font. For instance, you might describe Comic Sans as *fun*, *childish*, and *handwritten*. Even if you have never seen Comic Sans before, the scrawled feeling of the irregular shapes and angles of the letters will call such adjectives to mind. Understanding the visual aspects of written texts requires that we pay attention to the shape and the feel of the typeface itself.

What adjectives would you associate with the following typefaces?

Bauhaus 93

Broadway

COPPERPLATE GOTHIC

Kunstler Script

Forte

Times New Roman

As you consider the font, think about any treatment or formatting applied to it. For example, how has capitalization been applied? Are the words in *sentence case* (standard capitalization for a sentence) or some other case?

> Sentence case appears with an initial capital letter and a period at the end.
>
> all lowercase is written in all lowercase letters.
>
> ALL CAPS IS WRITTEN IN ALL CAPITAL LETTERS.
>
> mIxED cAsE iS a mIxTuRe oF cApItAL aNd LoWeRCaSe leTterS.

What do you associate with each of these capitalization styles? In academic writing, sentences are usually presented in sentence case, and all caps is usually used only for headings or subheadings. In informal, creative, or multimodal texts, all caps might be used for emphasis or to signify "yelling" or some other strong emotion.

When considering the features of words, check for typographic elements, such as text set in bold, italics, quotation marks, color, or different sizes or text set with strikethrough or highlighting. Each of these elements shapes the way readers interact with the text. Words that convey a warning, for example, might be set in red, a color associated with fire and stop signs. If different font sizes are used in a text, readers will assume that larger words are more important than smaller ones.

MM2-c Purpose and audience: What is the purpose of the written words? Who is the intended reader?

Take a look at the text on the next page, a letter by Gerald Gainley, the CEO of Canyon Cove Chemicals. The company wants to expand its facilities; however, the local government has blocked that expansion because of concern over environmental damage and unchecked

LETTER WRITTEN TO A SPECIFIC AUDIENCE

Dear Springfield and All of the Supporters of Canyon Cove Chemicals:

I write to you to convey my dismay and disappointment with the city council, our elected governing body.

Earlier today, as you may know, the city council, under the leadership of Stanley Burris, decided to block the development of a new Canyon Cove Chemicals refining facility on Oak Wood Road, just ten miles north of our city center and north of the city offices in which this decision was made.

This decision was prefaced by a self-serving, self-promotional, unnecessarily accusatory statement made by Council Chair Burris, who attacked Canyon Cove Chemicals.

Canyon Cove Chemicals has been devoted to and supportive of our local community for more than seventy-five years. We have sponsored the little league teams on which our children have played. We have donated funds to build the playgrounds and skate park at which our youngsters enjoy outdoor activities. We have allocated a part of our annual revenue to supporting our high schoolers in continuing their education at our two area community colleges.

For Council Chair Burris to accuse the company of greed and overdevelopment is not only a travesty but also a threat to our fine community.

Better facilities for Canyon Cove Chemicals will mean more revenue and will provide our company with the ability to participate even more in supporting our community.

"I PERSONALLY GUARANTEE THAT CANYON COVE CHEMICALS, IF OUR FACILITIES EXPANSION MOVES FORWARD, WILL DONATE TWICE AS MUCH IN THE COMING YEAR AS WE DONATED LAST YEAR."

I will stake my reputation and the reputation of the company I so proudly run on this claim.

Gerald Gainley
CEO, Canyon Cove Chemicals

industrial growth in the area. In response, Gainley distributed this letter to the local media and posted it on the company's Web site.

Why do you think Gainley wrote this letter? What was his purpose in writing it? The CEO addresses the letter to the entire city ("Dear Springfield") and "All of the Supporters of Canyon Cove Chemicals," indicating that he hopes to maintain support for the company despite the fact that it suffered a bad outcome in a city council vote. To be successful, his message needs to appeal to the general public and especially to readers who work for the company, support the company, or are active in local government (as representatives and voters, for example). The letter has to ease their concerns and draw attention to the benefits the company brings to the city. Think about the choices Gainley makes as he tries to accomplish those goals. Consider his words as well as their typographical treatment.

In the letter, Gainley uses two different fonts. Comic Sans looks handwritten and is rarely used in professional communication. Times New Roman is a more standard font, often used in newspapers, books, and other publications. What message does each font convey to the reader? Comic Sans might not be an effective choice for someone who wants to be taken seriously, but a handwritten font does underscore the personal feel of Gainley's communication—he is speaking on behalf of the company, but he's also speaking as someone who has a personal stake in the company and the community. Think about how the effect of the text would be different if all of the words were set in Times New Roman.

Note Gainley's capitalization choices as well. Some statements are in sentence case, and others are in all caps (see p. MM-17). How do you think the CEO wants readers to feel about the all caps statement in quotation marks near the end of his letter? Formatting the statement in all caps adds emphasis and might be intended to convey Gainley's commitment to the words. Perhaps the quotation marks are meant to show that his promise is a quotable statement—one he expects community members to hold him to.

Consider also what the letter is *not*. It's not a television or radio spot. Why do you think Gainley chose a letter to the city to convey his message? Why do you think he sent the letter to local television and radio stations and posted the letter on the company Web site? Gainley could have paid to run television and radio ads to convey this message. Perhaps he felt that a written statement would have a more personal, sincere feel; the letter format allows him to address all residents of Springfield and the surrounding area directly—including those who work for the company or have family members who have benefited from the company's local donations and support. Why do you think he chose not to include any images? He may have felt that

a picture would draw attention away from his words or that a picture of himself or the proposed new facility might make it harder for readers to think of him as their peer. His repeated use of the phrase *our community* makes it clear that he counts himself a citizen, not just the head of a company.

MM2-d Meaning: What effect do the words have on the reader?

Given what you know about Gainley's written statement regarding the city council's vote against Canyon Cove Chemicals' plan for expansion, what do you think of Gainley's chosen mode of expression—written words—and his decisions about how to present those words? Do you think his letter had the desired effect?

In an essay for his communications class, student—and Springfield resident—John Nikolakakis wrote the following analysis of Gainley's letter:

> In his letter to the city of Springfield, Gerald Gainley, the CEO of Canyon Cove Chemicals, expresses his "dismay" and, at times, disgust at a recent city council decision, in which the members voted against allowing the company to expand its facilities in north Springfield. He characterizes the city council members as shortsighted and essentially accuses them of putting the city in peril; that is, he doesn't say it directly, but he does imply that the company could move to another city, and then Springfield would lose the support and economic donations of the company. Gainley also makes an interesting promise to the city of Springfield.

> Gainley makes two textual choices that are worth attention: his use of fonts and his use of all capital letters (ALL CAPS). Gainley has formatted his letter almost entirely in Comic Sans. The font looks handwritten and may be perceived as bubbly and childish. Some of Gainley's critics have charged that the use of Comic Sans in this situation is inappropriate. If he were writing more formally, that criticism would be totally on the mark, but he wants the letter to be personal and to make him seem like a friend to its readers. The average Springfield citizen, Gainley's audience, will likely feel that the font is approachable and appropriate for a personal appeal.

> Interestingly, one sentence in the letter is not in Comic Sans. When Gainley pledges that Canyon Cove Chemicals "WILL DONATE TWICE AS MUCH IN THE COMING YEAR AS WE DONATED LAST YEAR" if the company is allowed to expand its facilities, the promise is set in Times New Roman and ALL CAPS. Both of these formatting choices show that Gainley wants the statement to stand out from the

rest of his letter and carry an official weight; he regards these words as a solemn oath to his readers.

When you analyze written words, it's important to consider the composer's choices of document type, font, and formatting. These choices may enhance or work against the composer's intended message. As you develop your own interpretation of the overall meaning of the text, think about how genre, features, purpose, and intended audience affect the reader's experience.

ACTIVITY MM2–1: Your understanding

Find a campaign banner or bumper sticker from a campus, local, or national election. Write a paragraph in which you analyze the features of the text you've selected. What font is used? What meaning does the font convey? What methods of emphasis are used with the text (for example, boldface or underline)? Think about the intended purpose and audience for the campaign piece and determine what message the text and the piece as a whole convey about the political candidate.

MM3 Analyzing sound

Sound is everywhere. Birds chirp, cars honk, music plays. Sometimes it's just in the background, but sometimes it's used for deliberate effect. Think about how sound functions in gambling casinos. Until recently, slot machines dispensed coins to winners. The noise of coins dropping from the winning machine was deliberately magnified so that other gamblers would notice and be encouraged to continue gambling. Most casinos have shifted to a receipt-based system—the machine generates a receipt that a gambler can turn in for cash. Because the sound of coins dropping out of a machine is so effective, however, machines still make that sound, even though no coins are involved. Sound can convey meaning on its own or enhance meaning when combined with other modes. When analyzing sound, consider the questions in the chart on page MM-22.

MM3-a Genre: What kind of sound is it?

Although we're surrounded by sound, we don't give it much thought most of the time. Even the music we listen to is often just background for other activities, unless we're studying music. But sound influences those who can hear it, even if they're not fully aware of the effect.

Analyzing sound

Genre

What kind of sound is it? Is it speech, music, or a noise associated with a particular object, for example?

Features

How would you describe the sound? Is it loud or quiet? Does it have a high or a low pitch? Is its pacing fast or slow? Is it in the background or in the foreground? Are certain sounds louder or quieter than others?

Purpose and audience

What is the purpose of the sound? Does it provide atmosphere? Is it accompanying something else, such as an image? Or is it the main or only mode of communication?

Who is the intended audience for the sound? A single listener with headphones? A room full of people? Children or adults? Experts or nonexperts? Sympathizers or opponents?

Meaning

How do genre, features, purpose, and audience work together to convey a message? How do you interpret the use of sound? (Keep in mind that your interpretation—your take on the meaning—may differ from the composer's intended message.)

Consider the music in a movie, which usually consists of the score (original music composed for the movie) and licensed music (clips from songs or orchestral works, for example). After you watch a movie, a few catchy tunes or notes might stick in your head, but for the most part you won't be able to describe what the music was like throughout the movie. And yet successful music will affect the way you perceive the entire film. A trumpet solo might make a scene or character seem more heroic, for example. Soft music might encourage viewers to feel thoughtful in a somber moment. Loud, fast-paced music might accompany a chase scene to enhance the sense of speed or urgency.

Music is just one type of sound that can be part of a movie soundtrack. To think about how sound as a whole functions in a composition such as a movie, you first need to identify what kinds of sounds are involved. A soundtrack can include dialogue—one or more people talking. It can also include sound effects—sounds associated

with particular animals or objects, such as birdsong to signal morning or cars honking to provide a busy urban atmosphere. And the music might be a scene-setting background melody or part of a performance happening on the screen. You can use these categories to identify types of sounds in audio-only or multimodal compositions and to examine what purposes individual sound elements serve in a larger composition.

In movies, sound often provides a supporting role. Unless it's dialogue, sound is usually in the background, enhancing the action on-screen. What about sound in compositions that are strictly audio? A podcast, for example, can be an audio-only file designed to be downloaded from the Internet and listened to on a computer or portable music player.

In one composition class, students were asked to create a podcast on a compelling local issue. Before they wrote or recorded anything of their own, they analyzed podcasts created by other students. First-year student Talia Souza chose to analyze a podcast titled "Hustlers, Street Vendors, and Farmers," in which the author, King Anyi Howell, visited a Los Angeles farmers' market geared toward black customers. Souza knew she wanted to do something related to food and farming, and she was interested in Howell's focus on selling food in one community. Howell's podcast offered a rich mix of spoken text and background sounds for Souza to analyze.

Souza listened several times, first for content, then a second time to take careful notes on the content. The third time through, she listened for the various background sounds and made some notes on the podcast as a whole:

Narration by Molly Adams (welcome and intro)

Then upbeat, jazzy music (horns and drums?) plays under Molly's voice

Music fades out as Molly introduces the piece

King Anyi Howell's piece starts with the sound of two men talking, outside—can hear what sounds like car traffic and people walking by; can hear the rustling of one of the men putting something in a bag; can hear the men talking about the cost of what's being bagged

Howell's voice comes in over the two men talking, explaining that he's at a farmers' market

Howell describes the busy intersection (can hear street sounds in the background)

Howell introduces a young woman, a shopper who describes the market

ONLINE   **hackerhandbooks.com/multimodal**
> Multimodal resources > Podcast
> King Anyi Howell, "Hustlers, Street
Vendors, and Farmers"

> Howell describes a group of vendors, with men talking in the background
>
> Sounds in piece: narration (by writers); clips of people talking; music; street noises

Whether you're analyzing sound in conjunction with other modes (when it's used in a movie, for example) or on its own (as in an audio podcast), it's a good idea to listen to the soundtrack or audio track several times. So that you can focus on the sound, do not take notes until the second or third time you listen. If there are layers of sound (talking in the foreground and street noise in the background, for example), first examine those elements separately and then think about how they work together.

MM3-b Features: Examine the pitch, pace, and volume of the sound

When analyzing sound, you'll also want to consider qualities like pitch, pace, and volume. *Pitch* is a measure of the highness or lowness of sound. A child's voice, for example, is often high-pitched, whereas a lion's roar is low-pitched. In speech, pitch provides inflection, which affects how listeners interpret the words being spoken. A statement that pitches upward at the end usually sounds like a question. If you've seen the movie *Ferris Bueller's Day Off*, you probably remember the scene in which a teacher (played by Ben Stein) takes attendance. The teacher's monotonous delivery of the students' names reflects his overall persona in the classroom: flat and boring. The camera pans to show his students falling asleep before class has even begun. This serves as a humorous justification for Ferris's skipping class.

Pitch can offer valuable clues about what's happening in a segment or piece. When people become frightened or stressed, the pitch of their voice tends to go higher. Higher pitch in movie music can emphasize anxiety and fright on-screen and inspire those feelings in the audience.

In addition to pitch, think about pace and volume when analyzing sound. Does the sound seem to be fast or slow (*pace*)? Is one sound louder or softer than another (*volume*)? Does the pace or volume of a particular sound change? What is the effect of any changes on the listener? In the movie *Jaws*, pace and volume work together to create suspense. A simple set of tones plays when the shark is near. These tones get faster and louder as the shark gets closer to an unsuspecting swimmer, encouraging a sense of panic in the audience.

MM3-c Purpose and audience: What is sound being used for? Who is the intended listener?

When people use sound to convey a message, they usually make deliberate choices based on their intended message and the listeners they're trying to reach. When you analyze sound, it's important to think about the composer's choices. Consider King Anyi Howell's podcast, described on page MM-23. Why did Howell choose to create a podcast rather than make a movie to be watched or write a story to be read? Perhaps Howell imagined that a single listener, surrounded by the sounds of the podcast, would be more absorbed in the story than a viewer distracted by images on-screen or a reader with only words on paper to consider. A listener has to imagine the images; the background sounds Howell provides along with the spoken story makes those images vivid and absorbing.

MM3-d Meaning: What effect does sound have on the listener?

When you analyze sound, it's important to consider the composer's choice of sounds and the pitch, pace, and volume of those sounds. These choices may enhance or work against the composer's intended message. The following is an excerpt from Talia Souza's analysis of sound in King Anyi Howell's podcast, which Souza wrote in preparation for creating her own podcast.

This podcast is hosted by Molly Adams, who provides a brief introduction with upbeat, jazzy music playing in the background. When the introduction is over, the main podcast begins. In it, King Anyi Howell uses three types of sounds. The first is human voice. Howell narrates the podcast, explaining the scene to listeners and interacting with the people he recorded for the podcast. He also includes segments of people talking, interacting with each other, and responding to his questions.

The second type of sound is background noises, which include street sounds that help set the scene: car engine revving, cars whooshing by, plastic grocery bags crinkling, and change jingling. The third type of sound is music playing. Rather than using recorded studio music, Howell includes the sounds of live music being played at the farmers' market, so listeners can hear not only the music but also other noise, such as people talking. This makes the music feel more authentic and shows how the music is part of the market scene. At the end of the podcast,

Adams provides a conclusion, and the lively, jazzy music plays underneath her voice again.

What I took from this podcast that I want to apply in my podcast is to interview people and include other people's voices. It's one thing for me to say that people believe a particular thing or hold a certain opinion, but it's more compelling to include other people's voices saying what they believe. This worked really well in Howell's podcast. Also, music and sounds can enhance a podcast and help listeners better imagine a place. Right now, my plan is to do a podcast about the dining options in the student union and how healthy they are (or aren't). If I record in the student union and interview people there, it will help my listeners imagine the space. Another aspect I liked was that Howell included a clear introduction and conclusion. I don't want someone else to do my intro and conclusion, as Adams did in Howell's podcast, but I like the idea of setting up the main part of the podcast and then concluding it at the end.

Although a composer's choices about the type of sound and its qualities are usually deliberate, they don't necessarily convey the same meaning to all listeners in all contexts. They may not work the way the composer intended, or they may carry additional meanings the composer didn't anticipate. As you develop an interpretation about the meaning of sound on its own or as part of a multimodal piece, be sure to consider genre, features, purpose, and audience together.

ACTIVITY MM3–1: Your understanding

Online movie trailers, used to advertise and preview movies, are approximately three to four minutes long. Television ads for movies are typically much shorter and limited in terms of how they grab viewers' attention and condense the story line. In your Web browser, conduct a search for "movie trailer." Scan the results and select a movie trailer to watch. Choose a full-length trailer so that you'll have more audio material to work with for this activity.

Close your eyes and listen to the trailer; do not watch it. Closing your eyes will allow you to focus on just the sounds. As you listen, identify the different sounds you're hearing and think about what function they serve, what feelings they evoke in you, how they are sequenced together, and so on. Then watch the trailer. You'll hear the sounds, see the sequences of images, and perhaps begin to note how they fit together. As you play the trailer a third time, create a list—somewhat like Souza's list on page MM-23—of the different sounds you hear. Once you have a list, identify each sound by genre and think about how the sound helps convey meaning in the trailer. Create a chart like the one on page MM-27 to record your notes. Consider adapting the chart and using it to document sounds in the different types of texts you study.

STUDENT NOTES ON A *SHREK* MOVIE TRAILER

Time	Sound	Purpose
:02-:10	man singing with symphony-like music	establishes context; creates opening for trailer
:11-:20	prince talking to big mirror hanging on the wall, mirror talking back; crowd of knights gasp	helps to set plot; prince's voice is kind of pompous-sounding; sound of gasps creates sense of disbelief
:21-:22	knight smashes small mirror	shows that prince is malicious! sound of mirror shattering contrasts with the opening singing/music
:23-:24	knight turns back to talk to big mirror	establishes a threat!
:25-:33	different symphony-like music with voice-over explaining plot of movie	continues to explain plot of movie; narrator's voice-over rhymes and feels storytelling-like

MM4 Analyzing static images

On any given day, you'll encounter images on billboards, road signs, maps, posters, flyers, brochures, product packaging, logos, advertisements, and so on. Images are all around us. Whether they're selling a product, conveying a message, sending a warning, or informing us about a law, they all have something to say. Although often we don't consider them carefully or critically, most images are designed to plant ideas or influence our decisions. When you want to analyze an image—to pick apart its message and how it works—think about the questions in the chart on page MM-30.

MM4-a Genre: What kind of image is it?

One of the first things you'll want to do when analyzing a static (or still) image is to determine what kind of image it is. Certain types of images do certain work and should be used for specific purposes. Consider the images in the chart on pages MM-28 and MM-29. The genre of each example is given along with a common use for each type of image.

Think about an image you see every day—perhaps a billboard or subway map you see on your way to work or class. What type of image is it? What does it mean to you? How might it work differently—or not work at all—if it were a different type of image?

Genre: What kind of image is it?

Photograph

Photographs can be used to represent specific places, people, or things.

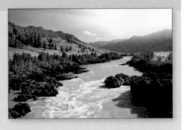

Sketch

Sketches provide an artistic rendering of places, people, or things.

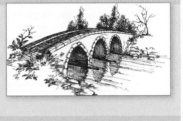

Map

Maps show specific locations or routes to locations.

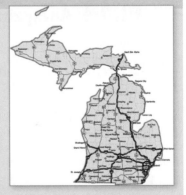

Clip art

Clip art can provide generic representations of a places, people, or things.

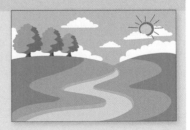

Sources (top to bottom): Straga; Danussa; Jami Garrison; Sapik.

Chart

Charts provide data in a format that is easy to read at a glance.

Diagram

Diagrams can be used to represent parts or functions of an object or process that are not usually visible.

Source (for both images): US Geological Survey.

Take a look at Figure 4–1, an image included in a set of instructions for applying women's hair dye. The image is a sketch, meant to represent any woman who might use the hair dye. If a photograph of a particular woman were used instead, viewers who look nothing like her might not be able to relate to her. But by using a sketch with generic features, the manufacturers are inviting all prospective users to imagine themselves following the instructions and using the hair dye carefully.

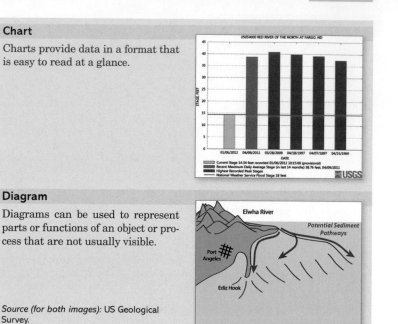

FIGURE 4–1 IMAGE ACCOMPANYING A SET OF INSTRUCTIONS. (*Source:* RetroClipArt)

Analyzing static images

Genre

What kind of image is it? Is it a photograph, cartoon, painting, map, chart, or diagram, for example?

Features

Is the image in color or black and white? In what context does the image appear? For example, is it large format (perhaps a poster) or small format (such as food packaging)? If the image has depth, what elements are in the foreground and the background? What is the perspective of the image (is it a close-up or an aerial view, for example)?

Purpose and audience

What is the purpose of the image? Is it accompanied by other modes, such as sound or written words? Or does it convey meaning on its own? Is it meant to teach, guide, warn, entertain, or provoke the viewer?

Who is the intended audience for the image? Someone zooming by in a car with only seconds to process the message? Someone who will spend time examining the image? Children or adults? Experts or nonexperts?

Meaning

How do genre, features, purpose, and audience work together to convey a message? How do you interpret the use of the image? (Keep in mind that your interpretation—your take on the meaning—may differ from the composer's intended message.)

MM4-b Features: Examine the context, perspective, and elements of the image

As you analyze an image, think about the context in which it appears. In other words, what surrounds the image? Is it an illustration in a book, a photo in a magazine, a warning in a building or vehicle, a painting in a gallery? How is the image presented? Do you have time to look at it, or do you need to absorb its meaning quickly? Does it need to be interesting, or straightforward? Should it make you want to buy something, find out more about something, or avoid something?

Think about images in product instructions. Because consumers usually want the assembly or use of a product to be as simple as possible, instructions typically use basic or generic images to illustrate steps, tips, or cautions. It can be difficult, however, to convey a clear message with a simple illustration.

In a technical writing course, students were asked to select a set of product instructions and choose one image from the instructions to analyze. Working with a one-page instruction sheet that came with an electric blanket he had recently purchased, Arman Chavva focused on the image of a dog's head with a circle and slash drawn over it.

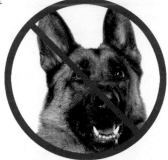

The image I chose to analyze in this set of instructions appeared in a list titled "Instructions for Use." The image was next to item #17, "Do not use with pets."

I chose this image because it is ineffective. The image shows a specific breed of dog, so a literal translation might be "no German shepherds." "No German shepherds" does not mean the same thing as "Do not use with pets."

Source: Boffi.

The technical writer who created the instructions was right in using the circle and slash, which in most cultures means "NO" or "DO NOT." However, the writer should probably have used a more general image to send the message of "pets." A photograph of a specific breed of dog doesn't send a general message. Instead, the author could have used simple shapes or clip art of a bird, a cat, and a dog, with the circle and slash over the shapes. The simple shapes would make users think of animals in general rather than one particular animal or one particular breed of animal.

In addition to thinking about the context of an image, you'll want to consider its perspective. All images present a point of view.

The extreme low-angle shot of a dandelion in Figure 4–2 challenges our notions of this summertime weed. The photographer has shot the dandelion from underneath—from the point of view of the grass or the earth—and has made it look majestic rather than mundane.

It's often helpful to think about perspective and elements of an image together. These are often referred to collectively as the *composition* of the

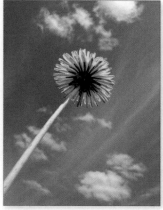

FIGURE 4–2 PHOTOGRAPH SHOWING AN UNUSUAL PERSPECTIVE. (*Source:* Dleonis)

image. If the image you're analyzing is a photograph of a man, you should ask yourself whether the man appears close up or far away. Is his whole body in view, or is only part of him visible? Are you viewing him head-on, from the side, from above, or from below? What about other elements in the photo? Is the man in front of, behind, or surrounded by anything? How do the perspective and the elements affect your impression of the man in the picture? For example, if the perspective makes it seem as though you're viewing him from above and perhaps through a door frame, he may appear powerless or even trapped.

Consider, for example, the well-known photograph *Migrant Mother*, taken by Dorothea Lange in 1936 (Figure 4–3). The woman looks slightly to the side of the camera; her eyes don't meet the viewer's gaze. Her expression might be troubled, but she doesn't look to the viewer (or the photographer) for help. She is surrounded by her children, whose faces are turned from the camera and buried in her arms. It is also worth noting what's *not* in the photo. We don't see a father or any other adults. These absences lead us to believe that this woman cares for these children alone.

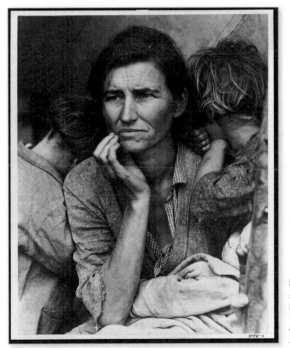

FIGURE 4–3
MIGRANT MOTHER **BY DOROTHEA LANGE,** 1936. (*Source:* Library of Congress/Farm Security Administration)

MM4-c Purpose and audience: What is the image meant to convey? Who is the intended viewer?

Think about the perspective and the elements of the *Migrant Mother* photograph. Why do you think the photographer took this photo? What is the photographer's purpose? What is your overall impression of the scene? Many viewers will conclude that the woman in the photograph represents strength in the face of hardship and despair.

Part of analyzing an image involves asking *Why did the artist create this image*? Sometimes responses to this question are left to interpretation; at other times, however, determining purpose can mean doing research. A bit of research would reveal that Lange was one of a number of photographers commissioned by the US government to travel throughout the United States and document the lives of Americans during the Dust Bowl in the 1930s. Her photographs, which captured the poverty and despair of people uprooted from their homes, were intended to inspire and educate. But inspire and educate whom? It could be said that her audience, or intended viewers, were both contemporary Americans not directly affected by the ecological disaster and future generations. Asking *why* and *for whom* can be helpful in determining the message and the meaning of an image.

MM4-d Meaning: What effect does the image have on the viewer?

As you develop an interpretation about the meaning of an image on its own or as part of a multimodal piece, be sure to consider genre, features, purpose, and audience together. Although a composer's choices about the type of image and its features are usually deliberate, they don't necessarily convey the same meaning to all viewers in all contexts. They may not work the way the composer intended, or they may carry additional meanings the composer didn't anticipate.

Consider student writer Ian Washburn's analysis of two news photos showing the toppling of a Saddam Hussein statue in 2003, during the United States' war with Iraq.

> The two photos tell two different stories about what happened in Firdos Square in Baghdad in April 2003. At the time the event occurred, I was stationed nearby in Baghdad. Major media outlets, including BBC, CNN, Fox News, and others, ran photos like the top image in fig.1 [see next page]—showing a cheering, chanting, supportive crowd. The US government itself shared some photos from a similar perspective.
>
> Later, however, other photos from the day emerged on the Web, like the bottom image in fig. 1, which some bloggers and commentators used as proof in claiming that

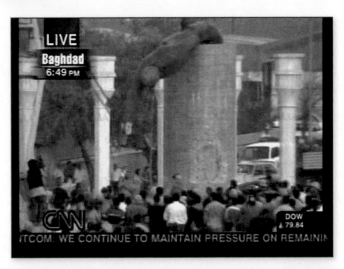

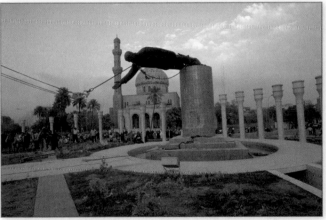

Fig. 1. Two views of the toppling of a Saddam Hussein statue, Baghdad, 2003 (UPI/Newscom; Nickelsberg).

the toppling of the statue was a staged "media event." What is clear in these pictures is that US tanks were stationed at each exit into and out of the area and that the crowd was pushed close to the statue and photos were shot primarily from behind the crowd, to create an illusion of a very big gathering (estimates indicate that about a hundred Iraqi citizens were there for the toppling of the statue).

The event did happen, and the event was important in the war against terror. However, the ways that the photographs were taken and presented tell a different story about *how* the events happened that day.

In his analysis, Washburn interprets the differences in the images by studying both the perspective and the point of view of each. He also hints at the purpose of the image in his discussion of the initially released photo. Examining static images in this way helps the viewer think carefully about a composer's message and consider possible meanings.

ACTIVITY MM4–1: Your understanding

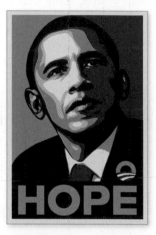

Source: Shepard Fairey

This image of Barack Obama originally appeared on posters during the 2008 presidential campaign. Consider the context of the image. How was this image used? How was it distributed? In what larger cultural and historical context was it important? Who was the intended audience?

Next think about how the image was transformed by various artists in other contexts. Consider the following examples. (You may find additional examples online by conducting an image search with terms like *obama* and *hope* and *poster* and *remix*.)

What effect does each image have on the viewer? Who do you think is the intended audience for each image? Why do you think the artists chose to invoke the Obama campaign poster when creating each of these images? What can you find out about the cultural and historical context in which these images were created?

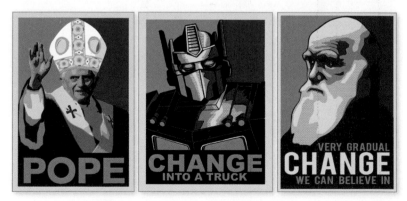

Sources (left to right): Michael Ian Weinfeld; Timothy P. Doyle; Mike Rosulek

MM5 Analyzing moving images

Today almost anyone can make a video and post it to YouTube. The opportunity is fairly new, however; before the Web and digital cameras, much of the video seen in an everyday context was "professional grade"—television shows, television ads, and movies, for instance. Today's composing tools allow users to craft moving images that can range from animated GIFs to moving type to digital video; the technology for making video has changed, and the term *moviemaker* is broader than it used to be.

The images in Figure 5–1 were created in 1887 by Eadweard Muybridge. To create the sequence of images, Muybridge placed a series of cameras in a row, with strings attached to the shutters. As the horse's legs hit the strings, a photo was snapped. In sequence, the photos show the physical movement of a galloping horse. This example is not necessarily a "moving image" as we think of it today, but it is the first photographic representation of a sequence of movement. What started out as a bet between friends—*Does a galloping horse ever have all four hooves off the ground at the same time?*—led to the birth of a new technology.

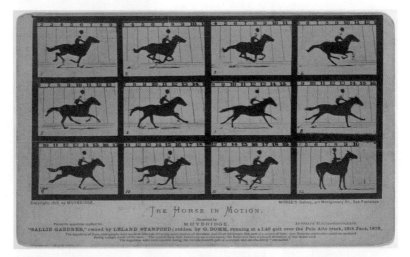

FIGURE 5–1 A SEQUENCE OF STILL IMAGES THAT REPRESENTS MOVEMENT. (*Source:* Library of Congress Prints and Photographs Division)

Analyzing moving images

Genre

What kind of moving image is it? Is it a feature-length film, a brief home-shot video clip, an animated sequence in a video game?

Features

What is the viewer's perspective? How are the elements of the images arranged? Do the images change quickly or slowly? Are any special effects used? How are the moving images combined with sound or words?

Purpose and audience

What is the purpose of the moving image? What did the composer hope to achieve with it?

Who is the intended audience? A viewer watching alone on a computer monitor? A large audience in a theater? Consumers? Students?

Meaning

How do genre, features, purpose, and audience work together to convey a message? How do you interpret the use of elements in the moving image? (Keep in mind that your interpretation—your take on the meaning—may differ from the composer's intended message.)

Today moving images entertain us, inform us, teach us, and encourage us to spend money. When you start to look critically at moving images, consider the questions in the chart above.

MM5-a Genre: What kind of moving image is it?

When it comes to moving images, the term *genre* can be used to describe thematic differences among feature films, such as "adventure" or "romantic comedy" or "documentary." Using terminology like this provides a convenient way to classify movies.

Because your examination of moving images may go beyond feature films, however, this section uses the term *genre* to discuss format rather than theme. Moving images can range from simple animated sequences to complex full-length movies. The chart on page MM-38 defines common genres.

Common genres (types) of moving images

GENRE	DESCRIPTION
Flip book	A physical animation created by drawing the same figure with slight changes on multiple pages and then flipping the pages to create an illusion of motion.
Simple animation	A computer-based animation using a series of still images and applying software techniques to make the images appear to be moving.
Stop-motion animation	An animated video effect created by moving an object a small amount at a time, photographing it each time, and then sequencing the images together to create a sense of movement.
Photo-realistic animation	Animation created through complex drawing, drafting, and computer rendering. The movies *Toy Story* and *Shrek* are examples of this kind of animation.
Playable animation	Animation sequences created by software designers and programmers for the specific purpose of interaction by viewers or players. These can be as simple as banner ads that change when viewers hover a cursor over the ad or sequences in longer video games.
Video clip	A short video that is typically created with a cell phone camera or a digital camera and posted, often unedited, to a site such as YouTube. Some video clips are edited before posting, especially those used for instructional or news purposes.
Film	Usually a feature-length motion picture, or movie. Perhaps the most common genre of moving image, film is used to bring fiction and nonfiction to life for entertainment and education.

MM5-b Features: Perspective, composition, and editing

As you analyze moving images, think about features such as perspective, composition, and editing. As a viewer of the moving image, you occupy a certain perspective. When viewing an instructional video, you are often the novice or student watching a teacher or trainer who walks viewers through a series of steps or a process for doing something. When you play a video game, you are often one of the characters in the game. Typically when you watch a movie, you are an observer, completely outside the action of the moving images. Perspective influences how viewers perceive what's happening on-screen.

For an assignment that required students to choose a movie and analyze one production aspect or element, Ellen Yin chose *Cloverfield*, a moving image that offers viewers an unusual perspective. The following is an excerpt from her essay.

> For most movies, the audience is supposed to be unaware of the camera. Viewers are supposed to have an experience of watching the movie and forgetting the existence of a camera filming and a stage, set, crew, and director. When we watch the Harry Potter movies, it's as if we're there observing the changes in the characters. When we watch *Transformers: Dark of the Moon*, it's as if we're there witnessing the battles between the Autobots and the Decepticons. The 2008 movie *Cloverfield*, however, was shot in a way that differs from most major movies; *Cloverfield* was shot primarily from a first-person perspective. The premise of the movie is that viewers are watching footage captured on a digital video camera found abandoned in New York City after the recorded action. This choice has a huge impact on viewers. Rather than being something we can overlook, the camera becomes a key element in the experience of watching the movie. The viewer feels as if she or he is holding the camera. By offering this first-person, handheld, low-quality perspective, *Cloverfield* forces viewers to join the main characters in their fight for survival.

Cloverfield is an example of a movie shot from a first-person perspective—making viewers feel as if they are there, experiencing the action themselves; the camera functions as the viewers' eyes (see Figure 5–2). This technique is sometimes called a *point of view perspective* or *subjective viewpoint*.

Another type of perspective is called *third-person view*. Video games often use this perspective: The "camera" is above and behind the player character, providing a bird's-eye view rather than the character's point of view.

Another quality of moving images to consider is the composition, or the artist's arrangement of the elements of the image—the

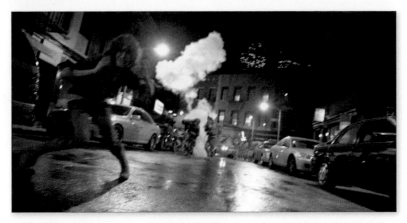

FIGURE 5–2 POINT-OF-VIEW PERSPECTIVE FROM THE MOVIE *CLOVERFIELD*.
(*Source:* Moviestore Collection)

people, props, products, and landscape. As a viewer, you might think critically about whether the people in the video seem close to or far away from the camera or close to or far away from other people. Or perhaps there are no people at all. Besides the frame of the movie, TV, or computer screen, can you find other "frames" as well—a window, perhaps, or an archway? Which on-screen elements seem to be emphasized in some way? Also consider what's *not* on-screen. Thinking carefully about what the composer may have left out of a scene could prompt an interesting analysis.

Professional film and TV producers use editing—choosing and sequencing shots—to craft a story and elicit a certain response from viewers. Some amateur video is edited (video-editing software can be inexpensive and easy to learn), and some isn't—usually depending on the composer's purpose and access to technology. When analyzing moving images, consider how editing affects the pace of the action and the narrative. Does the action proceed quickly from one shot to the next, as in a chase scene in an adventure movie? Or is the action more continuous? Does it proceed more slowly, as in a scene in which a character is shown deep in thought and gazing out a train window?

MM5-c Purpose and audience: What are the moving images being used for? Who is the intended viewer?

Creators of moving images make deliberate choices based on their purpose, or reason for creating the work, and on the viewers they're trying to reach. Thinking carefully about a composer's choices can

help you understand the work and also help you prepare for making your own choices as a composer of similar works. It's important to ask both *why* the composer decided to convey a message with a moving image and *what* message a composer is trying to convey.

Think about a national news broadcast, for example, which usually involves some combination of desk reporting, field reporting, and presentation of feature reports that were filmed and edited before the broadcast. Why are the various stories handled differently? Why do the producers decide to use moving images to present certain topics? Perhaps previously filmed material is needed because reporters can't get access to the subject at the time of the live broadcast. Maybe the story requires clips from a variety of sources for support, and those can't be pieced together on the spot. Or showing action is more likely to elicit an emotional response than showing a still image while a reporter narrates an event.

Filming and editing ahead of time also allows composers to shape the story for their target audience. Anything that might bore or offend the audience can be removed, and anything that's particularly effective can be emphasized. Next time you watch an edited news feature, think about who the intended audience is and how the feature has been shaped to reach that audience. Take a filmed, edited story about rising gas prices, for example. Many such features include at-the-pump interviews. What do you see in the moving image? How would you describe the people being interviewed—their gender, race, clothing, age? What kinds of cars are they driving: sports cars, minivans, cars in good or poor repair? Do they appear to be driving to work or taking a road-trip vacation? Are they smiling or frowning? Are they holding anything in their hands? Try to describe the feature's target audience—viewers most likely to identify with the people being interviewed. Would the audience identify as closely if only still images of drivers and gas pumps were used to support the story? Asking *why* and *for whom* a moving image has been created can be helpful in determining its message and meaning.

MM5-d Meaning: What effect do the moving images have on the viewer?

Although a composer's choices about the type of moving image and its features are usually deliberate, they don't necessarily convey the same meaning to all viewers in all contexts. They may not work the way the composer intended, or they may carry additional meanings the composer didn't anticipate.

Read an excerpt from student writer LeShawn Carter's analysis of a theme in *American Beauty*, a full-length film he viewed in an introduction to film study course. Carter is careful to consider the director's technical choices and composition in his analysis of the scene.

> Sam Mendes's *American Beauty* has no shortage of scenes in which the camera work and mise-en-scène suggest that the characters are trapped. Lenny Burnham is shown, for example, encased in window and door frames and is tightly framed by the camera. One scene in which the eye seems to get a break is the plastic bag scene, which we're supposed to see as beauty and perhaps freedom as we watch a plastic bag dance around in the breeze. The bag seems to move freely, but in fact the bag is not free at all. Mendes shoots the scene so that the bag is still constrained by the wind and the wall. It tries to escape but is pulled back into the shot again and again—reinforcing the theme.

As you develop an interpretation about the meaning of a video, an animation, or a film, be sure to ask questions about the genre or type of moving image, its features, and the purpose and audience for which the text was composed.

ACTIVITY MM5–1: Your understanding

Public service announcements (PSAs) are advertisements meant not to sell a product but to encourage or discourage particular behaviors or to call an audience to action (to contribute to a political campaign or to recycle, for example).

Search online for the original 1980s "brain on drugs" PSA, sometimes called the "fried egg" PSA. This PSA was shot from a first-person perspective. In the PSA, we are looking down as an egg is broken into a pan and begins to fry, while a voiceover says, "This is your brain on drugs."

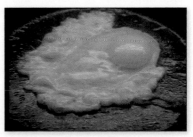

Source: Partnership for a Drug-Free America

Next search for an updated version of the PSA released in the 1990s, starring then-popular actor Rachel Leigh Cook. In this ad, Cook is the narrator. Rather than a first-person perspective, this version is shot more typically—viewers watch Cook smash the egg and then destroy the kitchen in which she appears.

Why do you think each of these techniques was chosen? Which do you think works better? Would the impact or effect of the older PSA be different if it had been shot with an actor and as a scene? How so? Would the impact or effect of the newer PSA be different if it had been shot from a first-person

perspective, as if the viewer were the person smashing the egg and destroying the kitchen?

What other advertisements—either public service advertisements or ads for products—have you seen shot from a first-person perspective? Were they effective? Why or why not?

ACTIVITY MM5–2: Your understanding

Most moving images we see are not interactive. That is, we watch them or somewhat passively receive the content. Some artists and advertisements, however, have thought a bit more creatively and innovatively about inspiring interaction with moving images.

The following still images are from a Skittles online ad campaign. In each of the ads, the viewer is invited to place his or her finger on the screen, at the spot indicated by the candy. The moving image that then plays is interactive with the viewer's finger. Do a Web search to find other ads from this campaign. What difference does the interactivity make? How does the ad feel different, or how do you respond differently to it, because of its interactive nature?

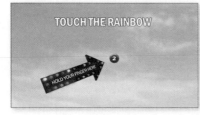
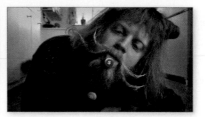

Source: BBDO Toronto; Wm. Wrigley Jr. Company

≣ MM6 Analyzing multimodal texts

Though the discussions in sections MM2 through MM5 each focused on a single mode, many of the examples in those sections were actually multimodal texts—texts that communicate with some combination of written words, static images, moving images, and sound. Look back at the brochure (image b) on page MM-16. The discussion in the text focuses on how words are arranged in different types of documents, but the brochure includes images as well. This section addresses analyzing different modes *together* in a multimodal composition, a task that is not as daunting as it may seem. On some level, you think about multimodal texts every day, simply because most texts *are* multimodal. Recipes and food packaging often include words

Analyzing multimodal texts

Genre

What kind of multimodal composition is it? An article with words and images, for example? A short film with sound and moving images?

Features

What modes (written words, sound, static images, moving images) are present in the composition? How does each mode work individually? How do the modes work together?

Purpose and audience

What is the purpose of the multimodal composition? Is it intended to provide information or argue a case, for example?

Who is the intended audience? The general public? Teenagers? Retirees? Professionals in a particular field?

Meaning

How do genre, features, purpose, and audience work together to convey a message in the multimodal composition? How do you interpret the combined effect of the modes used in the composition? (Keep in mind that your interpretation—your take on the meaning—may differ from the composer's intended message.)

and images. Television commercials usually include words, sound, and moving images. Even children's books, with words and illustrations, are multimodal.

When you start to look critically at multimodal texts, consider the questions in the chart at the top of the page.

MM6-a Genre: What kind of multimodal text is it?

Not only do people encounter multimodal texts every day, but they also create them every day. Personal photo albums with captions, slide shows with images and audio voice-over, social media posts with images and words—these are just a few common genres of multimodal composition. Different genres afford a composer different opportunities for sharing and shaping a message. For example, someone who wants to provide categories and subcategories of information might build an informational Web site, especially if the

Common genres of multimodal compositions

GENRE	DESCRIPTION
Informative Web site	Informative Web sites usually present statistics, research data, definitions, or other factual information. The Web site format allows composers to provide a large amount of information in manageable categories. A public transit Web site might, for example, have separate pages for timetables, maps, and policies.
Artistic video	Composers use artistic videos to present ideas on personal, political, environmental, and other themes. The video format allows composers to control the sequence of ideas.
Instructional video	Instructional videos often demonstrate steps for learning, creating, or installing something. A furniture manufacturer may, for example, provide an informational video to demonstrate the step-by-step assembly of a chair.
Slide presentation	Composers typically use slide presentations to present ideas and information in small chunks and in a particular sequence. A presenter might use slides to show how a proposed business plan could lead to corporate growth, for example.
Print advertisement	Print advertisements often occupy all or part of a page in a magazine, journal, or newspaper and can be used to promote products, services, or events. Because their space is limited and most readers won't spend more than a few seconds looking at them, print advertisements need to present key information at a glance.
Television commercial	In general, television commercials promote products, services, or events. Usually less than a minute long, commercials often rely on jingles and slogans to engage the viewer and convey their message in a quick, memorable way.

material doesn't need to be viewed in a particular sequence. If the order of information is essential, the composer might choose instead to create an informational video, to ensure that no one views the material out of order. When you're analyzing multimodal compositions, identify the genre and ask yourself why the composer chose that genre. The chart on page MM-45 shows common genres of multimodal compositions.

MM6-b Features: Which modes are represented? How do they work on their own and with each other?

When you analyze a multimodal composition, thinking about each mode on its own can be a helpful first step to interpreting the composition as a whole. Ask yourself what modes are present. Written words and static images? Audio and moving images? Then consider the role of each mode within the composition. What work does each mode do? For example, do written words convey information or make a plea? Does audio evoke an emotional response? Do moving or static images illustrate a concept or provide background?

Remember to consider the features of each mode as well. Are written words large or small? Bold or fine? Where do they appear? What size are the images, and how are they arranged? How are moving images sequenced? How loud or quiet is the audio? If you consider the modes separately, you'll be better equipped to think about how they work together.

Take a look at Figure 6–1, a public service message commissioned by the World Wildlife Fund, a group devoted to protecting nature. The composition uses two modes: written words and a static image. Which mode grabs your attention first? For most viewers, the cheetahs immediately draw the eye. But why? Think about the surrounding space. The background focus is so soft that no other distinct objects appear, only a dark blur. The cheetahs, however, are in sharp focus in the foreground. Their striking spots stand out against the muted background. It would be easy for a viewer to glance quickly at the public service message and see nothing but an adorable photo of cheetahs, except for one thing: the tags on their backs. Marked with "S" and "XL," these are unmistakably clothing tags. What at first appears to be a touching scene of mother and cub becomes more sinister with the recognition of these tags. These animals are going to be used for clothing.

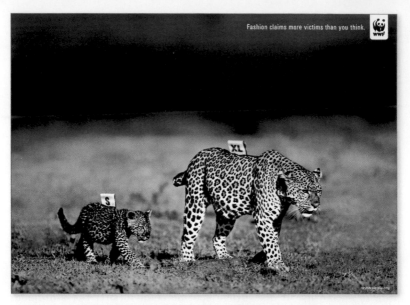

Fashion claims more victims than you think.

FIGURE 6–1 A PUBLIC SERVICE MESSAGE. (*Source:* World Wildlife Fund)

Student writer Wayne Anderson made the following argument about the ad:

The makers of the ad could have inspired outrage by showing a violent image of cheetahs that had been killed for their furs. They probably recognized, however, that many viewers would instinctively look away and try to forget the image rather than absorb the message. By emphasizing the image of the two cheetahs, the mother guiding her cub in their natural habitat, the ad designers draw in their audience and elicit a sentimental response. Some viewers will feel sympathy and want the cheetahs to survive.

The image alone, however, does not convey the whole message. It delivers a troubling truth and makes viewers feel sympathetic and sad, but it might not have a lasting influence. The text in the upper right corner adds a subtle punch: "Fashion claims more victims than you think." The statement plays on the familiar concept of fashion victims, people whose clothing choices make them look ridiculous. Here the term *victim* is being applied to the cheetahs that may be killed to gratify someone's fashion sense. If the image showed two adult cheetahs or an entire group, the image probably would not be as effective. It's easier for

most people to think of cubs especially as needing protection from harm. Maybe the term *victim* is supposed to make viewers feel protective and not just sympathetic. Playing on this familiar phrase also helps make the message memorable.

MM6-c Purpose and audience: What is the composition doing? Whom is it intended to reach?

When you think about the purpose of a multimodal composition, you might ask, *What is this composition meant to accomplish? Convey information? Inspire action or feeling? Make an argument?*

Thinking about audience, you might ask, *Whom is this meant to appeal to? Whom is this designed or written for? What assumptions is the composer making about the audience's beliefs and values?*

Consider again the two cheetahs. Why do you think the composers of that message decided to use the pronoun *you* in "Fashion claims more victims than you think"? Most public service messages aim to encourage or discourage specific behaviors. If the statement read "Fashion claims more victims than people think," it might be easier for the audience to dismiss the issue as someone else's fault or problem. Perhaps the composers hoped that addressing the statement to "you" would empower their audience to act — to refuse to buy furs or to spread the message. If the words are essential for reaching the audience, why do you think they're so small? Would the effect be different if they spanned the top or bottom of the image? Perhaps some viewers would feel alienated if they encountered the direct address (*you*) and the word *victim* before developing a sympathetic feeling toward the cheetah mother and cub.

Or take the example of restaurant menus. What is the purpose of a menu? The straightforward answer might be "to provide food options." But a menu might have other purposes as well: to differentiate a particular restaurant from its competitors, to show that the restaurant specializes in a particular type of food (for example, using the colors of the Italian flag or photos of pasta to show that the food is Italian), or to explicitly call attention to healthier menu options or options for people who have food allergies.

Who is the audience for a menu? The simple answer might be "hungry customers." But imagining how customers might encounter the menu reveals more about the intended audience. Although some customers viewing the menu might already be seated in the restaurant, others might be considering the menu online, trying to decide

where to eat dinner. In making their decision, they might be comparing the menu side-by-side with another restaurant's menu. They might be considering different factors related to their dining decision, such as how much money they want to spend on their dinner. Higher prices might indicate that the restaurant aims to attract an older crowd. Unusual font choices might mean that the restaurant seeks an eclectic audience.

For multimodal compositions, the actual audience might be much broader than the intended audience, so it's important to consider how and where the composition has been published. Student composer Marisa Williamson created a video essay, "To the Children of America," for a class. Though her intended audience was fairly limited — her instructor and her peers — her actual audience grew when she published her school project on a video-sharing Web site. Williamson's project is featured in sections MM7 through MM15 of this book.

MM6-d Meaning: What effect does the multimodal composition have on the viewer?

Although a composer's choices about the modes integrated into a multimodal composition are usually deliberate, they don't necessarily convey the same meaning to all viewers in all contexts. They may not work the way the composer intended, or they may carry additional meanings the composer didn't anticipate.

In the following excerpt, student writer Marley Cole analyzes item collecting in role-playing video games. Her attention to sound, images, and other features of the games leads her to disagree with one of her sources. In her essay, she includes both text and screen captures from in-game play to support her points.

> *Gamasutra* writer Kris Graft suggests that the desire to collect items in a game world is similar to compulsive hoarding in the real world. The consequences of gathering items may not be as negative for the gamer, but gamers and hoarders, according to Graft, experience similar degrees of emotional investment and gratification when they acquire objects. Graft, however, does not account for the limits placed on acquisition in many game worlds and the penalties incurred when the gamer ignores those limits. Usually, a character cannot carry more than a certain amount. Sometimes that amount increases when the character gets stronger, but there is always a limit. When the character's pack is full, that

character can't pick up new items (see the image on right for an in-game inventory example). The character is forced to discard or sell old items to make room for new ones.

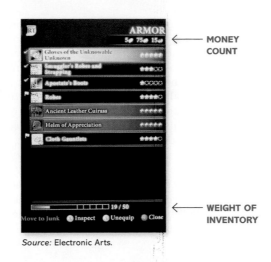

← MONEY COUNT

← WEIGHT OF INVENTORY

Source: Electronic Arts.

In some games, overburdened characters can't even move until they discard items. Rather than facilitating virtual hoarding, video games actually force gamers to be strategic about what they keep with them. In addition, the experience of parting with items is often positively reinforced. Selling an item can be accompanied by the sound of coins dropping into a pouch or the sight of a money count going up. A character who has lightened his pack might even be able to move faster.

Cole determines meaning by analyzing sounds and images in a multimodal text, a video game. As you develop an interpretation about the meaning of a multimodal piece, be sure to consider genre, features, purpose, and audience. Pulling together your individual impressions of the text's elements can help you look critically at the text as a whole.

ACTIVITY MM6–1: Your understanding

Many public service announcements (PSAs) are advertisements meant to encourage or discourage particular behaviors (such as voting or littering) or to call an audience to action (for example, contributing to a charitable organization).

Choose a nonprofit or community action or awareness organization. Find a campaign that the group has run or is running, and identify at least three different campaign components (such as a poster, a radio spot, a television PSA, a Web-based PSA, an interactive game). Analyze each of the three pieces, describing which modes are used, how the modes are layered together (or not), and how well you think each piece serves its purpose.

Some historical and contemporary campaigns you might look at include Rosie the Riveter, wildfire prevention, ready.gov, Make a Wish Foundation, and the Humane Society. You might also focus on the World Wildlife Fund campaign mentioned in MM6-b.

MM7 Starting your own multimodal project

Sections MM2 through MM6 focused on analyzing individual and multiple modes in the works of others. Sections MM7 through MM15 will help you think about your own multimodal composing. As you develop your own project, you'll want to keep genre, features, purpose, audience, and meaning in mind, just as you do when you analyze. Think about questions like these as you plan and compose:

Genre: What kind of composition do you plan to create? A video? A Web site? A poster with images and written words? (Depending on the genre, you may need to budget more time for the assignment, brush up on technical skills, or collaborate with others.)

Features: What kinds of images, colors, design elements, fonts, and type treatments are appropriate for your composition? What would make your composition most effective? Adding voiceover narration or including information in callout boxes, for example?

Purpose and audience: What does your composition need to do? Does it need to inform, instruct, argue, entertain, or persuade? Whom does it need to reach? Novices who need basic information? Experts who need to see detailed support? Children who would respond well to a colorful presentation? People who agree or disagree with you?

Meaning: What message do you want to convey? What is the goal of your project? How do your chosen genre and features help you achieve your purpose and reach your audience?

Keep in mind that you may not be able to answer all of these questions before you begin gathering information and drafting. The answers you come up with early on may change as you investigate your topic and begin to build your project. It's a good idea to revisit these questions throughout your composing process.

MM7-a Getting direction from the assignment

The composing process often begins with an assignment, which may provide answers to some of your questions about genre, features, purpose, audience, and meaning. Take a look at this assignment about binge drinking, for example:

Design a six-panel brochure that persuades college students not to binge drink. Your headings and body text—along with any graphs, diagrams, or photos—should work together to define the term and discuss the dangers of binge drinking.

The assignment provides the topic—binge drinking—and requires a specific multimodal genre—a brochure with images and written words. It also provides a general purpose—to persuade—and a target audience—college students. It's up to the student to determine the specific message. For example, *Binge drinking can lead to health problems that plague drinkers long after college* or *One night of binge drinking can be fatal and isn't worth the risk.* The student will need to think about what features will help make that message persuasive. What colors, typefaces, and images, for example, will be appropriate for the message?

MM7-b Considering the "So what?" question

If the assignment does not specify a topic, choose one that allows you to explore a genuine interest or address a real concern your audience may have.

Effective composers take stock of their own goals and the needs of their readers, asking *What, aside from a good grade, motivates me to compose?* Make sure you have a reason for composing—a reason that addresses the "So what?" question. A project that stems from genuine motivation will be more engaging to your audience. One student writer made a chart to help her decide how to respond to this prompt: *Persuade fellow students to take your side in a campus debate.*

SAMPLE STUDENT NOTES: DECIDING ON A TOPIC

Possible topic: Should the college convert two acres of campus green space to additional parking spaces for commuter students?	So what?	Hm. I'm not a commuter, so it's not that critical to me.
Possible topic: Should the college publish the school newspaper in an online format only and abandon a paper publication?	So what?	Seems like a no-brainer to me. We're all on our devices 24/7 anyway. And going online only is greener, right?
Possible topic: Should the college add a general education requirement that each full-time student must complete a minimum of 12 hours of community service by the end of the second year?	So what?	Volunteerism should absolutely NOT be required. I can convince fellow students that a requirement goes against the concept of volunteering—of giving back out of a sense of goodness. Plus, being a college student means making your OWN decisions.

The student chose this topic because she cared about it, felt her readers would care about it, and felt she could make compelling points to support her views.

You need to consider the "So what?" question even if your purpose is not to persuade or argue. If the assignment is to demonstrate a process for instruction purposes, think about what you can bring to that project that will make it especially clear or helpful. Your audience will see value in your work if you are invested in it.

MM7-c Understanding expectations and managing your time

Even if the assignment is detailed and clear, you'll probably have questions for your instructor as you get started. You'll want to consider questions like these, which are typical of almost any writing assignment:

- Do you need to run ideas by your instructor before you get started?
- Will you have time in class to work on the assignment?
- How can you break your project down into manageable steps?
- What sorts of research should you do? Should you conduct field research, such as interviews? Or should you focus on library sources, like books and journal articles?
- Are you working on your project alone? With a partner? Or with a group?
- How will the project be evaluated?

You'll also want to consider additional questions, however, that relate more to the multimodal aspects of the project, such as the following:

- Can you include images, videos, or sound clips in your composition?
- If you want to include links in your essay, how should you present those links?
- Where can you go for help if you've never created a multimodal composition before?
- What options do you have for sharing drafts and getting feedback if your project is a large file or in several pieces?
- If your final project is a large file, how should you submit it?
- How should you present a list of works cited for something like a video or a podcast?

Getting answers to questions like these before you begin your project can help clarify some of the details of your project and ensure that the project starts smoothly.

ACTIVITY MM7–1: Your understanding

Before moving further, take some time to view the two student projects discussed in sections MM7 through MM15. (Visit the URL at the bottom of this page.) One, an informative Web site, offers an overview of loose leaf tea. The other, a video essay, explores how YouTube helps young people experience events of the past. How are these compositions multimodal? Identify some of the successful features of each.

ACTIVITY MM7–2: Your project

Review a monomodal writing assignment you recently completed or a piece of writing you composed on your own (a traditional five-page academic essay, perhaps). Imagine if you had been asked to produce the composition as a multimodal piece instead. What genre would have been effective for your purpose, audience, and message? A slide show? A movie? A Web page? A collage? Consider some of the materials you might have drawn on to craft the piece as a multimodal composition: audio, video, animation or movement, still images, and so on. Write briefly about what you might have done and why.

MM8 Considering your purpose and audience

Purpose is the goal of your work—your aim or objective. Your purpose will inform many of the decisions you make as a composer. Your audience is made up of the people who will read, view, or listen to your work. When you're composing in college, it's easy to think that your audience is limited to "the teacher." Yes, your instructor is part of your audience, but usually your instructor is not your primary audience or the only audience you are writing to.

Often, the assignment will suggest or require both a purpose and an audience. In a composition course, for example, an instructor might ask each student to use photos and written words to argue a position in a current campus debate. In a marketing course, the assignment might call for a slide show presentation that analyzes consumer trends over time. In a natural sciences class, the assignment might ask students to write and direct a public service announcement that informs viewers about hurricane preparedness. These are all examples of academic projects, but the purposes are different for each. In these examples, the composition student's purpose is to *argue*, the marketing student's purpose is to *analyze*,

ONLINE   hackerhandbooks.com/multimodal
> Multimodal resources > Student multimodal projects
> D'Amato, "Loose Leaf Teas"
> Williamson, "To the Children of America"

and the natural sciences student's purpose is to *inform*. If, for example, the natural sciences student produced a short digital movie in which he made an argument that state agencies need more funding for hurricane preparedness, he would probably not be satisfying the assignment.

Audience considerations also influence the content and presentation of your project. Sometimes your instructor will give you guidance about who your audience is—other students on your campus, for example, or state legislators. Sometimes the assignment will direct you to address a particular audience, such as student athletes or readers of your campus newspaper. If your purpose is to persuade, your main audience will probably be those who disagree with you or are undecided. If your purpose is to instruct, your audience will probably be nonexperts, those who need basic or step-by-step information.

MM8-a Prewriting with your purpose in mind

Student composer Alyson D'Amato was assigned to create an informative text—that is, a text that teaches readers about a topic. D'Amato began thinking about what she needed to do by reviewing the assignment for the project.

ASSIGNMENT FOR AN INFORMATIVE PROJECT

Think about the ways in which information is provided in our culture. Your assignment is to take a subject that's familiar to you and to compose a multimodal project that informs or instructs your audience or explains something to them. You can create a slide show presentation, a Web site, a brief video, or something else. Engage your audience, make your purpose clear, deliver your information, and provide enough examples so that your audience comes away with a good grasp of the topic.

From the assignment, D'Amato knew she needed to create an informative, explanatory piece. She knew that she was expected to produce a multimodal project. Her instructor invited students to choose a topic they were interested in.

When D'Amato received the assignment, she analyzed her purpose. Her initial notes looked something like this:

- explain something, provide information
- include pictures and words
- teach people about something new or unknown
- start with what I know and care about

D'Amato's instructor provided the initial, formal purpose for the project: to create an informative piece. D'Amato decided that she had to do some additional prewriting to help her determine why the topic mattered to her.

My purpose: Create something about brewing your own tea and teaching people how to do so. I love tea and make my own teas—I want to teach other people that making tea means more than dunking a tea bag in a mug!

- explain something, provide information
  - — capture audience's attention
  - — teach them to do something that might be new to them
- include pictures and words
  - — explain using text and use photos to illustrate the text
  - — use pictures to keep people's attention
  - — use pictures people can relate to (not too artistic or unrecognizable or anything)
- teach people about something new or unknown
  - — use language people will understand—like the newspaper
  - — explain terms that might be unfamiliar
- start with what *I know* and *care* about
  - — explain why it's important to me
  - — explain why it might be important to others—answer the "So what?" question!

It's fine to start out fairly broad, but before you begin drafting and creating, you'll want to have a strong sense of what you want and need to accomplish with your multimodal composition. D'Amato's notes provide a good model for how you might start thinking about your purpose.

MM8-b Identifying your audience's needs and perspectives

In the previous example, student composer Alyson D'Amato was asked in her assignment to "engage" her audience. To determine what the audience will find engaging, composers first need to *identify* an audience. Here are some questions you might ask as you think about who your audience is:

- Does the assignment provide any direction about who the audience is? What clues about audience has your instructor provided?

- Is there a particular audience you want to reach?
- Could you have more than one audience?
- What do you know about your audience's life experiences? Interests? Demographics (age, race, socioeconomic status, level of education, location)?
- What are the most effective ways to engage your audience members—attract their attention, get them interested, help them learn, and so forth?

Finding answers to these questions will allow you to see your topic from your audience's perspective.

Sometimes professionals in marketing or product development will create "profiles" of different types of people who make up their intended audience. These profiles help them to imagine specific details behind a general idea like "audience." For a project in a technical writing class, students were asked to write a proposal for a new, Web-based application to be used by their peers at the university on the school's Web site. To get a sense of the possible audience for their Web-based app, a group of students worked together to create user profiles. They interviewed other students and came up with two user profiles.

Group 1   One potential user group is made up of residential students who are online at least 7 hours a day and who primarily use Facebook to stay connected with friends. These users visit Web sites only to seek information not available through Facebook. They use the college Web site to look up their class schedules and check grades and sometimes to look for news about what's going on around campus. One student told us: "If there was a way to sync up the college Web site with Facebook, that'd be great!"

Group 2   Another potential user group is made up of commuter students, many of whom have transferred from a community college. They live off-campus and are not online as often as those in the first user group. Most work at least part-time and use the Internet primarily for work-related e-mail and projects. This group typically uses the college Web site only when enrolling for classes. One student told us: "I guess I'd need a reason to use the school site more."

You might create a similar profile for your audience. Or you might just do some brainstorming in answer to questions like these:

- Where are your readers/viewers/listeners from?
- When were they born?

- What groups or causes are they involved with?
- What experiences have they had with your topic?
- What are the best ways to reach them?
- How are they likely to receive your message?

NOTE: When creating profiles of your potential audience members, keep in mind that people are diverse. Creating audience profiles is helpful when it gives you a sense of the people you are trying to reach and what they are interested in and value. Your profiles should not turn into stereotypes that lead you to make faulty assumptions that homogenize or alienate your audience.

MM8-c Connecting with your audience

With your purpose in mind and your audience profile under way, you are ready to think about the best way to connect with your audience. The benefit of composing multimodally is that you have options for communicating your message. Consider the following scenarios and think about what decisions you would have to make to best connect to these audiences (highlighted).

- You are composing for a group of local second graders to teach them about air quality.
- You are composing for other college students to share advice on making sound financial decisions.
- You are composing for your school's administration to propose building a war memorial on campus.

How can you appeal to these audiences in these situations? The second graders, for instance, might need pictures to help explain the concept of air quality. The college students might be interested in hearing audio clips from other students who have faced specific financial challenges. You might reach the school administrators by knowing the school's mission statement and core values and presenting slides that connect those values to your proposal.

When student composer Marisa Williamson began working on her composition, she did some talking, reading, and exploring. Her assignment was to present an argument creatively on a topic of her choice and for an audience of her choice. She was familiar with writing argument essays; for this project, however, she decided to compose a video argument. Williamson wanted to explore historic events that had national attention in the United States and somehow tie them together. She wanted to connect to people her own age, so she began

by thinking about events from her own childhood that made a lasting impression on her and had national significance. The event that stood out most clearly was the September 11, 2001, terrorist attack that destroyed the twin towers of the World Trade Center in New York City.

Williamson realized that what she was thinking about wasn't an argument yet. She started to think about other national events that were captured on film or video, what they have in common, and what it means to her generation to experience historic moving images recorded before their birth. To brainstorm ways of effectively reaching her audience, she also thought about arguments that she had encountered that had affected her thoughts or feelings on a subject. This process helped Williamson start shaping her argument and planning her project.

MM8-d Recognizing an unintended audience

Keep in mind that your composition will sometimes have a broader audience than your purpose or your assignment suggests or than you intended to reach. Because multimodal compositions often live online or in some portable electronic format, they typically can be publicly viewed or shared. Someone who runs a Web search on your name, for example, may find your project. Your project may also have a longer life span than you intend. If you take down a Web site you've created, pieces of it may have been downloaded and shared elsewhere by others. Even if you're creating your project for a specific group of people, make sure your work is something you'd be comfortable sharing with a broader audience that may include friends, family members, or future employers, for example.

ACTIVITY MM8–1: Your understanding

Look around campus for a poster that catches your eye. It could be hanging in the financial aid office, in the writing center, on an instructor's office door, or even in the kitchen of the dining hall. Take a picture of the poster or sketch it out on a notepad to refer to later. Identify the purpose or purposes of the poster. What clues help you identify the purpose?

ACTIVITY MM8–2: Your understanding

Take a look at just the home page of the following sites:

- the main Web site for your school
- the Web site of a professor at your school

- the Web site of a fast-food restaurant in your area
- the Web site of a small, locally owned restaurant in your area
- the Web site of the company that made the car you drive or that makes the car you'd like to drive
- the Web site for a branch or an agency of the US government (for example, the White House, the IRS, the FBI)
- the Web site for an individual who serves in the US government (such as a member of Congress)

As you look at each home page, generate a list of notes about who you think the primary audience is for each Web site. How do you know that this is the audience? What information—textual or visual—provides clues about who the audience is?

ACTIVITY MM8–3: Your project

With a current project in mind—in any class—consider your audience for composing. Take notes on the following questions.

- What sort of information do you need to gather about your audience? How will you go about gathering that information?
- Your audience members might have specific questions that are pertinent to their needs. Can you anticipate what those questions might be?
- Some members of your audience might be resistant to or skeptical about your topic; you might need to appeal to them using different types of evidence. What kinds of evidence might work best?

MM9 Planning your project

Composing a multimodal project requires planning, and planning takes time. You'll have to settle on a process that works for you or, if you're collaborating with one or more classmates, that works for all of you. You'll also have to identify a main idea and the best genre (an inspirational video or an informative Web site, for example) for expressing that main idea. If the genre is not your choice but has been assigned, it will take planning to figure out how to best communicate the main idea in a particular type of composition. Planning is hard work, but it's also full of opportunities to think and rethink, shape and reshape your project.

Sometimes you will start a project in one direction—perhaps thinking something like *I'll create a Web page that teaches people how*

to tie fly-fishing lures—and find, as you do research and think about
your audience and purpose, that a video might be a better way to
instruct your audience. The good news is that you don't have to have
everything planned before you start to compose.

MM9-a Understanding your own composing process

Have you ever put together, or watched someone else put together,
a thousand-piece puzzle? Approaches for completing a puzzle vary.
Some people start methodically with the border. Others start with
a key image in the center of the puzzle and work outward. Still others work randomly, fitting together islands of puzzle pieces here and
there and eventually joining them. There's no right way; it's just a
matter of figuring out what method works for each puzzle and for the
person putting it together.

Composers, too, have their own preferred ways of working, so it's
important to think flexibly about the composing process. Sometimes
you'll see the composing process presented in a fairly linear way, like
this:

1. Brainstorm
2. Plan
3. Research
4. Compose
5. Revise

Those basic steps find their way into most projects, and the process
usually begins with brainstorming and ends with revision, but composers usually take each step more than once and at several times
throughout the process. Consider student composer Marisa Williamson's project: a video essay.

In talking with other people in her class and with friends,
Williamson found that all of them had seen iconic footage and
pictures from events in recent history, but few could remember
key words spoken about the events or by those involved in the
events. Based on what she knew about her audience, Williamson
decided—with rough ideas about her purpose and how to proceed—
to knit video clips, still images, audio files, and her own narration
together to make an argument that would appeal to her peers.
She used a video-editing application that allowed her to combine,
sequence, and edit all the materials she had gathered and also to
layer in text and titles.

A linear rendering of Williamson's composing process might look something like this:

1. Brainstorm about purpose and audience
2. Gather images and video
3. Choose songs
4. Write and record narration
5. Input images, audio, video, and narration
6. Add text
7. Produce video

Represented visually, Williamson's composing process might look something like Figure 9–1.

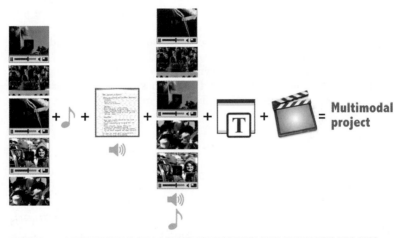

FIGURE 9–1 VISUALIZATION OF A LINEAR APPROACH TO THE COMPOSING PROCESS FOR A MULTIMODAL PROJECT.

This is a fairly neat and orderly way of visualizing the elements that are part of a composing process, and certainly these are important steps in the process. The way Williamson compiled, wrote, and thought through the different elements of her composition, however, might actually be better and more accurately represented visually as in Figure 9–2.

The student's composing process was not so much a linear path as it was a series of loops in which she revisited stages and elements of her composition. She began by gathering and watching different videos. She then selected some still images, collected some songs, and scripted her narration. Each of these pieces affected her thoughts about and presentation of the others. She went back to the video to edit it and to trim pieces, add to other pieces, and sequence

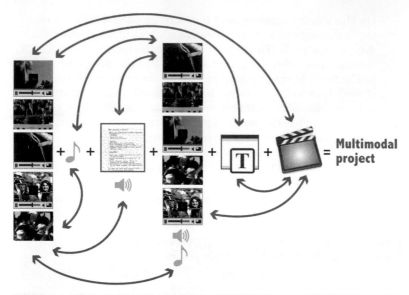

FIGURE 9–2 VISUALIZATION OF A REALISTIC APPROACH TO THE COMPOSING PROCESS FOR A MULTIMODAL PROJECT.

clips together. She worked with the music, trimming and editing and deciding how to layer it under her narration and on top of the video and images. She found different audio clips and replaced or changed the audio in the project. She did this over and over again, while she also continued to write and edit her script to reflect changes in the sequence of video pieces and images. What was essential for Williamson was budgeting enough time for the shaping and thinking and *re*shaping and *re*thinking.

MM9-b Collaborating effectively with others

Working in a pair or in a group can change your composing process — how you go about brainstorming, drafting, researching, and revising. The old saying is that "two heads are better than one," and composing with a group can be enriching. Collaborative work gives you an opportunity to explore ideas and practices that your peers bring to the project. It's also valuable practice for work you will do outside of school. Many professional projects are done in teams.

Collaborating effectively takes practice. It helps to pay attention to how you best work and how you best work with others. Here are a few important tips for working with a partner or a group:

Do the work together, and learn from each other. Sometimes students look at collaborative work as just a matter of divvying up tasks (for instance, one person does the research, another does the writing, and another does the designing and production). Managing a project in this way can result in a piece of work that looks somewhat like Frankenstein's monster—lots of pieces stitched together into a messy whole. Stronger, more coherent work is the result of people truly collaborating and working together on *every* aspect of a project. The process of doing so allows group members to learn from one another's strengths, and, in turn, everyone in the group becomes a stronger, more capable composer.

Organize yourselves, and stay on task. Functioning well as a group means checking in often and planning together. Three

Assessing your strengths as a collaborator

I am good at being a **team leader**.	yes	no	kind of
I am good at being a **team member**.	yes	no	kind of
I am good at **communication** (asking good questions and facilitating discussions).	yes	no	kind of
I am good at thinking about the **big picture** (staying focused on the main idea or goal of the project).	yes	no	kind of
I am good at thinking about **small details** (completing individual tasks and keeping track of smaller parts of the project).	yes	no	kind of
I am good at doing **research** (performing Web searches, gathering information from library databases, and conducting surveys or interviews with people).	yes	no	kind of
I am good at **design** work (working with or creating images, or thinking about layouts and color schemes).	yes	no	kind of
I am good at **writing** (brainstorming, drafting, and editing written materials).	yes	no	kind of
I have good **technology** skills (creating basic Web pages, making slide show presentations, and doing some work with digital video).	yes	no	kind of

ways to keep your group focused and make progress are to set up specific meeting times, to have someone take notes when you meet as a group, and to make sure everyone knows who's doing what for the project.

Know your own strengths, and be ready to admit your weaknesses. One way to start, especially if you're working with classmates you don't know, is to think about how you typically like to function in a team or a group. What do you do well? Individual members can assess their strengths by using a questionnaire (see the checklist on p. MM-64). The responses on the questionnaire can help you get to know each other and start a conversation about how to move forward.

MM9-c Deciding on a main idea

Just as well-planned essays begin with a working thesis statement, your multimodal project should have a main idea around which the entire composition is focused. And be sure that your main idea addresses the "So what?" question (see section MM7-b)—your main idea should be compelling and interesting and address a question or concern of interest to others. Having a main idea will help you select the best images, audio, and other elements to support that main idea. You may have to whittle away at a big, general idea to settle on a manageable main idea.

As you get started on a project, you'll likely have lots of ideas to explore. Sometimes it's tempting to stick with a broad subject. Most writers find, however, that doing so can actually be a problem, as there's too much material to cover and it's tricky to figure out how to approach the subject. "The World Wide Web," for instance, is a gigantic subject, but certainly a lot of academic writers get a lot of mileage out of projects about the Web. The trick is to ask questions about the subject in an attempt to narrow it to a topic and to find your particular angle, one that matters to you.

BROAD SUBJECT	The World Wide Web
QUESTION	*Great for shopping and communication, but what good is it doing in the world?*
NARROWER TOPIC	Using the Web during and after a disaster
QUESTION	*Where have we seen this? What has been the effect? Why is it important?*
MAIN IDEA	How Japanese citizens are using the Web as a tool for activism in the aftermath of the 2011 nuclear disaster and slow government response

Brainstorming ideas and then focusing and whittling down those ideas is a great way to get started. When student composer Alyson D'Amato started thinking about creating a project focused on tea (a broad subject), she came up with a list of possible angles:

organic tea	tea growing	history of tea
store-bought tea	tea brands or	tea flavors
black teas	companies	uses of tea
green teas	fair trade teas	bottled tea vs. brewed
tea and health	tea plants	tea
tea in different	tea popularity	serving tea (different
cultures	brewing tea yourself	rituals)

D'Amato knew that she couldn't address all of these possibilities in one project. Some of the issues—tea in different cultures, for example—seemed too complex for the scope of the assignment. Other ideas—store-bought tea, for example—seemed as though they might not be interesting for her or her audience.

She identified three possibilities from the big list she generated, and then she brainstormed what she might cover for each of those possibilities:

- black teas vs. green teas
  - focus on compare and contrast?
  - the differences in the plants
  - the differences in the flavors
  - the growing popularity of green tea
- serving tea
  - historical tools, like really old tea-serving pitchers
  - different cultural rituals (like "high tea" in England)
  - different types of ceremonies involving tea
  - from rituals and ceremonies to tea bags in a box bought at the grocery store
- brewing tea yourself
  - why do it when tea bags are so easy?
  - differences between tea bags and loose leaf tea
  - health benefits of tea
  - loose leaf tea recipes

Because she was so personally interested and invested in tea brewing herself, D'Amato decided to choose the third option, to

compose a project that would teach people about brewing tea. She knew she would further develop and refine her main idea as she researched her topic, but now she had a focused starting point. (See your handbook for more on narrowing a subject to a topic and more on developing thesis statements.)

MM9-d Planning support for your main idea

A multimodal project often gives you new opportunities for presenting evidence in support of a main idea. You may think of evidence only as quotations from sources or perhaps as data from experiments. Multimodal projects allow you to think more broadly. You can support your idea with quoted written words—but also with quotations in the form of podcasts and other audio files. You can include data in the form of graphs and tables—but you can also present data in animations. Support in a multimodal composition can take the form of words, images, audio/sound, video, and so on.

Think about the visual rendering of student composer Marisa Williamson's writing process in Figure 9–1 (p. MM-62). As the visual shows, she chose to mix images, video, and audio (speech clips, music clips, and her own narration) in her video essay. Since she was planning to argue the thesis that online video-sharing sites such as YouTube bring together people of different generations by letting viewers experience events of the past, she knew that her best evidence was going to be YouTube videos. She made a list of possible events to include.

John F. Kennedy's inaugural address	Iranian hostage crisis
Martin Luther King Jr.'s "Dream" speech	Geraldine Ferraro's candidacy
Assassination of John F. Kennedy	Assassination attempt: Ronald Reagan
Assassination of Martin Luther King Jr.	Birth of MTV
Assassination of Robert F. Kennedy	Space shuttle *Challenger*
Landing on the moon	Million Man March
Woodstock	September 11
Apollo 13 crisis	Hurricane Katrina
1976 Bicentennial	

Marisa's list included patriotic events, political events, cultural events, tragic events, and natural disasters. When she reviewed her list, she decided that she wanted to focus on just one of these categories of events. The event that resonated most strongly for her was

the September 11 attacks. She remembered the strong sense of unity that followed throughout the country. So she decided to focus specifically on tragedies that have brought people together in the past and connect generations now through YouTube footage. Even after making that decision, she felt she needed to whittle the list down to one or two tragedies for each generation, so that her audience could easily connect with what other generations had felt.

Since Williamson wanted her audience to be able to experience what each generation saw and heard as these tragedies occurred, she chose to include as evidence excerpts from iconic speeches (of John F. Kennedy, Martin Luther King Jr., Ronald Reagan) to layer over the images and videos. She could have chosen to support her argument—that YouTube provides much more than a casual distraction—with clips of people talking about how video-sharing sites have revolutionized the way we experience and *re*experience events. But she thought primary sounds would be more powerful, more convincing support.

As you mine for and select evidence for your project, keep your purpose in mind. What are you trying to achieve—and why? What types of evidence will help you do so convincingly? Also keep your audience members in mind—their age, experiences, biases, and needs. What kind of evidence will be most effective?

Be sure to evaluate any potential evidence for relevance (to your purpose and audience), authority, currency, and accuracy. You'll need to question whether a photo, a podcast, a video, or anything else you choose will be compelling and credible to your audience. See your handbook's section on evaluating sources.

MM9-e Choosing a genre; deciding on a delivery method

Deciding how to deliver your ideas is an important part in planning your project. First, you'll need to think about your audience and purpose: Whom are you composing for—and why? When you're mulling over how to deliver your ideas, you'll also have to think about the support you plan to include in your composition.

When Alyson D'Amato began to plan her project, she thought about the ways in which people would want to learn about her topic. She felt that a slide show presentation about brewing tea wouldn't be too interesting and wouldn't really fit her purpose, especially since most slide show presentations are designed to be delivered by

a speaker. She knew she wanted people to be able to easily access and use her information, and she knew they'd probably need to go through the information on their own.

She considered creating a video and was excited about the idea of actually recording herself talking about tea and making tea, but she wasn't sure how to include the recipes she wanted to share with her audience. To help organize herself as she considered different ways to convey the information, D'Amato created a table listing the pros and cons of different delivery methods (see p. MM-70).

D'Amato decided that a Web site would be the best way to share her ideas. With a Web site, she knew she could include written words and images, maybe embed video, and create an overall organization that would allow viewers to experience her site at their own pace.

Considering different formats, as D'Amato did, is an important part of your planning. For more on the technical aspects of delivering your project, see section MM15.

ACTIVITY MM9–1: Your understanding

Review a writing assignment you recently completed or a piece of writing you composed on your own. Imagine that it had been a collaborative, group project. How do you think your composing processes would have been different? What would you have learned or gained by collaborating? How might the project have turned out differently? What difficulties or opportunities might you have encountered if the project had been collaborative?

ACTIVITY MM9–2: Your understanding

Consider the broad subjects in the following list. Narrow each one by asking questions. Propose a manageable topic for a multimodal composition for at least two of the four subjects.

* The most recent presidential election
* Video games
* Social networking sites
* Environmental issues

ACTIVITY MM9–3: Your project

For a project you are currently planning, take some time to consider your own main idea. Is it narrow enough? Do you have a specific angle on the subject? Pair up with a classmate and share your idea. Pitch your plan for gathering support and seek feedback from your classmate. Are you planning the most convincing support for your main idea? Take notes from your conversation.

SAMPLE STUDENT NOTES: DECIDING ON A DELIVERY METHOD

Delivery method	Pros (+) and cons (-)
Slide show	+ Viewers can watch slides at their own pace and navigate back or skip ahead. + I can use images, written words, and links. + I can include any recipes I want to share. + I can use text animations to spice things up. - Slide show presentations often seem dry and not engaging. - The final file might be really large, and my audience would probably have to download it to view it. - To view my project, my audience might need to have the same slide show software I have.
Video	+ Video would seem cooler than a slide show. I could include a soundtrack with music and voiceover. + Actually watching someone make tea in a video might be more helpful than written instructions. + Video would allow me to control the sequence of information, but that's not really important to me for this project. - I'm not sure how I would include my recipes so that they could be saved and used. Maybe a download link at the end of my video? - I'd have to keep it short or risk boring my audience. - Video can be hard to edit. If I change any visuals, I might have to adjust the soundtrack.
Web site	+ A Web site would be easy to share. All I'd have to do is provide a URL. + Viewers would be able to control the order in which they see information and easily revisit things they find interesting. + I could include my recipes on the pages or as downloadable files. + I could include any image, audio, or video files I wanted to. + There are plenty of free Web site builders online that I can use.

☰ MM10 Managing your project

A huge part of imagining, drafting, creating, revising, and publishing a multimodal project is managing the pieces of the project. When you write a typical academic essay, you often work with only one piece: your document filled with written words. When working on a multimodal project, you might be managing two, three, four, or dozens of pieces, most if not all of which are electronic files. Each of these files likely has a different name and is of a different type. It's easy to feel overwhelmed when negotiating .wmv, .mov, .bmp, .m4v, .pdf, .jpg, and other files.

This section offers a few good practices for managing files across a multimodal project:

- Saving all your files in one place
- Keeping track of where your sources came from
- Using clear, descriptive names when saving your files
- Keeping track of versions when sharing your files with others

MM10-a Saving all your files in one place

Before you really dig into a project, decide where you're going to work on it. If your project is digital and will include images, audio segments, or movie clips, for example, that workspace is probably a folder on your computer. With multimodal projects, often the different components need to sync with or "talk to" one another. If one file is saved on your computer's desktop and another file is saved in a "My Documents" folder, the applications you use to compile your project might not be able to find all the files. And you might not be able to find all the files either!

When Williamson began gathering clips and working on her video project, she created a "Writing Class Project" folder on her USB drive. This was a useful initial storage space for all her files. You can see in Figure 10–1 that she has sound files, video clips, and some word processing documents stored in the folder.

Fairly quickly, however, Williamson realized that she needed to be more organized — by the time she had twenty files in her "Writing Class Project" folder, she found it was getting harder and harder to sort through all the files and find specific pieces.

She created three separate folders within her "Writing Class Project" main folder — one for music, one for video clips, and another

for audio clips (Figures 10–2 and 10–3). She left her word processing documents in the main folder because they dealt with the overall project, whereas the files in the subfolders were pieces of the larger project.

Williamson's file-saving strategy isn't the only way to save files for a major project, but she found that it worked well for her, and it's a good example of how you can create a file management system for a multimodal composing project.

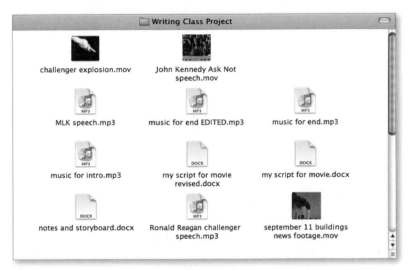

FIGURE 10–1 FOLDER FOR STORAGE OF MULTIMODAL FILES.

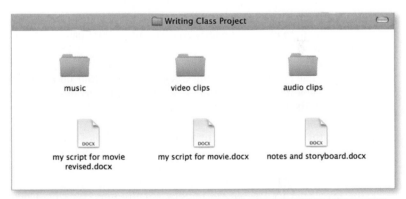

FIGURE 10–2 FOLDER FOR A MULTIMODAL PROJECT ORGANIZED WITH SUBFOLDERS FOR MUSIC, VIDEO CLIPS, AND AUDIO CLIPS.

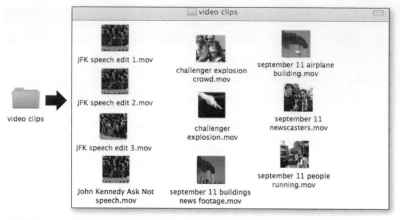

FIGURE 10–3 SUBFOLDER CONTAINING ALL THE VIDEO CLIPS FOR A MULTIMODAL PROJECT.

MM10-b Keeping track of all your files

As you brainstorm and research your project, gathering and selecting examples, resources, and other materials, you might think, "Oh, I'll remember where I found this!" But as you collect pieces from a variety of sources over a span of time, you will probably lose track of where you found at least a few things, and that can cause you problems further down the road. For example, if you use an audio quote in a draft of your project and later decide you'd like to include a few seconds more of what the speaker said, you'll have to find not only the original sound file but also the exact moment when the words you've quoted are spoken. Your job will be much easier if you've got the whole sound file in your project folder along with some notes about the speaker, where the file came from, when you downloaded the file, and the time stamp for the words you're interested in using. You may want to keep your notes in a list that provides key information about each of the files you're collecting.

Figure 10–4 shows part of a list Williamson kept in her "notes and storyboard" word processing document in her "Writing Class Project" folder.

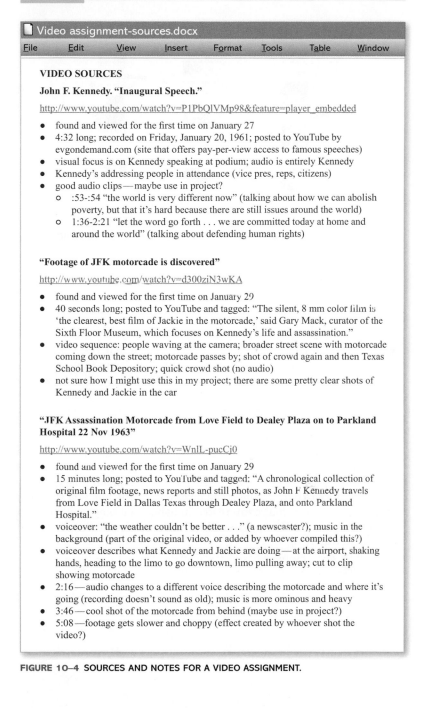

VIDEO SOURCES

John F. Kennedy. "Inaugural Speech."

http://www.youtube.com/watch?v=P1PbQlVMp98&feature=player_embedded

- found and viewed for the first time on January 27
- 4:32 long; recorded on Friday, January 20, 1961; posted to YouTube by evgondemand.com (site that offers pay-per-view access to famous speeches)
- visual focus is on Kennedy speaking at podium; audio is entirely Kennedy
- Kennedy's addressing people in attendance (vice pres, reps, citizens)
- good audio clips—maybe use in project?
  - :53-:54 "the world is very different now" (talking about how we can abolish poverty, but that it's hard because there are still issues around the world)
  - 1:36-2:21 "let the word go forth . . . we are committed today at home and around the world" (talking about defending human rights)

"Footage of JFK motorcade is discovered"

http://www.youtube.com/watch?v=d300ziN3wKA

- found and viewed for the first time on January 29
- 40 seconds long; posted to YouTube and tagged: "The silent, 8 mm color film is 'the clearest, best film of Jackie in the motorcade,' said Gary Mack, curator of the Sixth Floor Museum, which focuses on Kennedy's life and assassination."
- video sequence: people waving at the camera; broader street scene with motorcade coming down the street; motorcade passes by; shot of crowd again and then Texas School Book Depository; quick crowd shot (no audio)
- not sure how I might use this in my project; there are some pretty clear shots of Kennedy and Jackie in the car

".JFK Assassination Motorcade from Love Field to Dealey Plaza on to Parkland Hospital 22 Nov 1963"

http://www.youtube.com/watch?v=WnlL-pucCj0

- found and viewed for the first time on January 29
- 15 minutes long; posted to YouTube and tagged: "A chronological collection of original film footage, news reports and still photos, as John F Kennedy travels from Love Field in Dallas Texas through Dealey Plaza, and onto Parkland Hospital."
- voiceover: "the weather couldn't be better . . ." (a newscaster?); music in the background (part of the original video, or added by whoever compiled this?)
- voiceover describes what Kennedy and Jackie are doing—at the airport, shaking hands, heading to the limo to go downtown, limo pulling away; cut to clip showing motorcade
- 2:16—audio changes to a different voice describing the motorcade and where it's going (recording doesn't sound as old); music is more ominous and heavy
- 3:46—cool shot of the motorcade from behind (maybe use in project?)
- 5:08—footage gets slower and choppy (effect created by whoever shot the video?)

FIGURE 10–4 SOURCES AND NOTES FOR A VIDEO ASSIGNMENT.

MM10-c Using clear, descriptive names when saving files

File names like "audio piece" or "draft 2" don't mean much when you're working with and compiling lots of files. One way to manage your files is to use a descriptive and consistent naming system. For instance, you might decide to include the word *audio* in the file name of all your audio clips: "audio_opening_music" and "audio_jayne_talking."

You might also consider date stamping your files when you save them. Your computer does this automatically, but it helps sometimes to see the date in the file name ("writing project May 5" or "writing project 05_08_12," for example). Doing so will help you make sure that when you resume working on your project, you're working with your most recent draft. Date stamping can also help you avoid writing over earlier drafts, which you might need later.

MM10-d Keeping track of versions when sharing files with others

Part of managing files, especially when you work collaboratively, is developing a system for sharing files. It's easy, and frustrating, to end up with multiple versions of a file that have to be merged. Say, for instance, that you are working on a project with two other students, John and Chelsea. You each have a copy of your project. John is making changes to it, and Chelsea is making changes to it. Suddenly, you have three different versions of your project: yours, John's, and Chelsea's. Figuring out who made what changes and getting all of those changes into a single draft is difficult and time-consuming.

Passing around one file and working on that one file individually is a good approach. If you're passing around a file, make sure that only one member of your group works on that file at a time. Or try uploading the file to a collaborative workspace, so that all members of your group make changes to a single version. Whatever strategy you adopt, maintaining good communication with your group members is essential.

ACTIVITY MM10–1: Your understanding

Online tools that help you create, manage, and save files can be especially helpful when you're working with files you need to share with others. Look online for three such tools (GoogleDocs, for example) and generate a list of pros and cons for each. As you create your list, think about what criteria are important to you. Here are a few questions to help you get started:

- Does the tool let you save multiple files in one place?
- How large can the files be?

- What types of files are allowed? Documents? Audio files? Image or movie files?
- Do files remain posted until you take them down? Or do they expire after a set time?
- Does the tool allow multiple people to edit a file at the same time?
- Does the tool record information about who makes saved changes?
- Can you easily download the file after all changes have been made and saved?

ACTIVITY MM10–2: Your project

Come up with a file-saving strategy for a project you're about to begin. If you're already working on something, describe your current file-saving strategy and think about what's working well and what you might improve. Think about how you want to handle different types of files, for example, and how you want to manage your series of drafts.

MM11 Outlining and drafting your project

In section MM9, on planning your project, you saw a visualization of Marisa Williamson's writing process—a visualization that was not neat and orderly (see Figure 9–2, p. MM-63). In the process of working on her project, Williamson moved back and forth across the pieces she was developing and working with, selecting an image here, identifying a video piece to use there, revising her narration before recording it. Although Williamson's *process* might have seemed a bit haphazard, her final *product* is sequenced, polished, and very well organized.

Your ideas might be expressed in written words, in audio, in moving images, in still images, or in some combination. Regardless of the media you're working with, organizing your ideas before and as you draft will help you meet your goals as a composer and will help you meet your audience's needs.

MM11-a Choosing the right organizing tool for your multimodal project

How you organize the information you're presenting depends on the type of document you will produce and what different modes you might use. A slide show presentation, for instance, is typically linear.

Most slide shows have a title slide, an introduction slide or two, body slides, a conclusion slide, and so forth (see Figure 11–1). If you're giving background information or presenting a problem that needs solving, you will want to do so early in your slide presentation. If

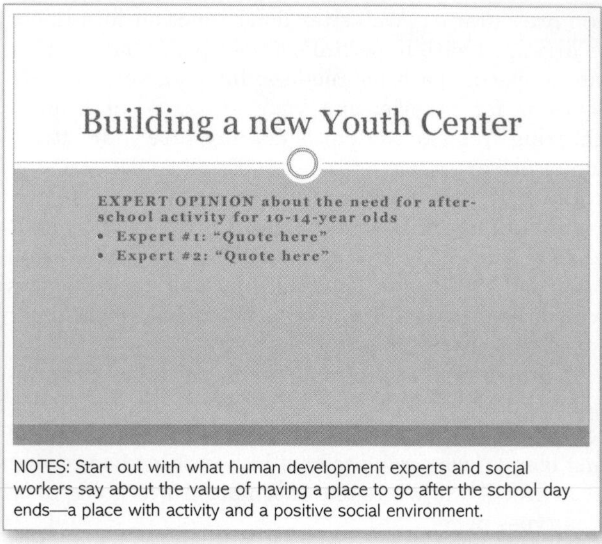

Template design allows the composer to focus on developing ideas instead of appearances.

The composer uses notes to plan evidence.

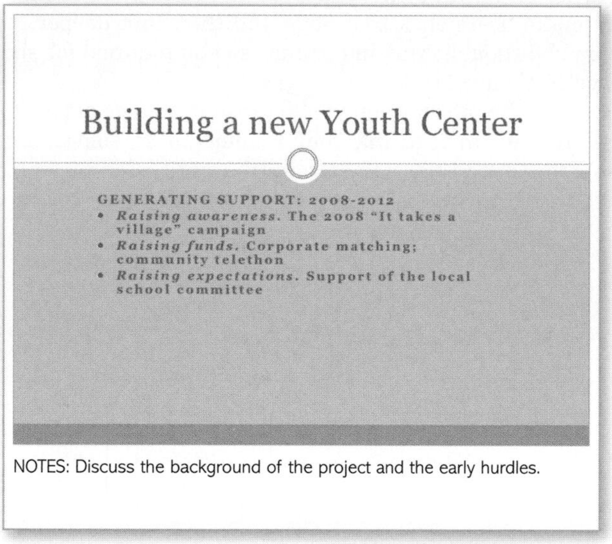

Notes help the composer create distinct goals for each slide.

FIGURE 11–1 DRAFTING A SLIDE SHOW PRESENTATION WITH NOTES.

you are giving reasons for support, think about how to arrange those reasons: Strongest first? Strongest last? The notes feature in Power-Point and other presentation software can help you as you play with arrangement and build your script. What also helps is that you can move slides around fairly easily. Slide show templates can help you figure out what information should be placed where.

Unlike a slide presentation, Web sites don't function in a linear way. They can be arranged with hyperlinks across pages, so you may not want to create a specific path for readers; instead, you can give them different options for experiencing your ideas. What is most important in organizing Web site content is making sure your categories of information are clear.

After Alyson D'Amato had considered her purpose and audience, determined her genre (an informative site), and started planning her content (brewing tea), she considered the different ways she could present information on a Web site. Having one long page readers would scroll down to read didn't seem ideal—nor did it seem to her like a good way to effectively create a Web page.

D'Amato decided to create a wireframe, or mock-up, of her project before starting to build her Web site. At first, D'Amato was going to have only three main links: to her tea story, to brewing tea, and to tea types. "Making blends" was going to be a link within the brewing tea page, and black, green, and white tea information was going to be linked from the tea types page.

She decided, however, that she didn't want to bury all of that information and make users click to a page and then link deeper to get to information she thought was important, so she planned for six main links, shown in Figure 11–2.

How you organize the information you're presenting also depends on your purpose. If you are teaching your readers to do something new, you will probably need to provide straightforward, step-by-step,

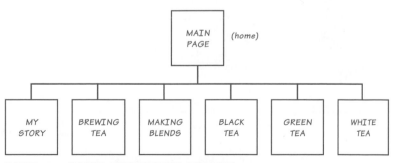

FIGURE 11–2 REVISED WIREFRAME FOR A WEB SITE.

numbered instructions. If you are composing a video essay that inspires people to reflect or to take action, you may have more flexibility in arranging your information for impact.

Once you have a strong sense of your topic and main idea and you've begun to assemble support, you'll want to think about organizing your ideas. Often for traditional essays, instructors focus on creating outlines, where you begin with a thesis statement and then develop the key ideas you will express in the body of your paper. Creating an outline is also an effective way to get started on a multimodal piece, because regardless of what you choose to include and how you choose to share information, it's crucial to have some guiding organization—a skeleton that you can flesh out in a draft.

Other tools can be useful for organizing your ideas. For instance, moviemakers often use a storyboard to think about how they will express ideas. A storyboard provides a space for a composer to describe the scene being set, any text that will appear on the screen, and the music or other sounds that will be in the scene. There's also room for the composer to add specific notes and a place for describing a transition (see Figure 11–3).

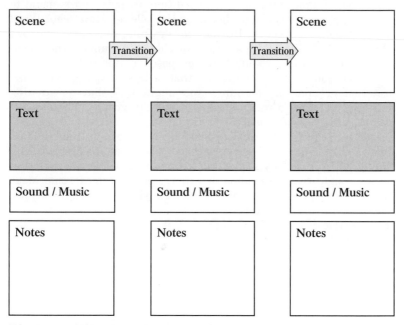

FIGURE 11–3 STORYBOARD FOR A MULTIMODAL PROJECT, WITH SPACE FOR THE SCENE, TEXT, SOUND OR MUSIC, AND NOTES.

MM11-b Drafting to support your main idea

Once you've settled on a main idea and sketched some sort of outline (or wireframe or storyboard), you'll need to gather and select the content that will best support that main idea. This is a good time to take another look at the assignment. Reread the requirements and the prompt(s) to which you're responding.

There's nothing magical about drafting. It takes time, of course, and it helps to have notes about your main idea, your evidence, and your organization close by. Successful drafters ask, anticipate, and respond to questions as they work through a draft, whether they realize it or not. A writer who is composing an instructional booklet may ask, for example, *How do people learn something new?* or *How did I learn to do what I'm trying to describe?*

Think about creating a multimodal document that teaches people how to plant trees. Your main idea might be "A healthy tree starts with a proper planting." You know your audience will want to know what constitutes "a proper planting." You decide there are steps, but how many steps? What's the first step? Once you start fleshing out the steps—considering the climate, assessing how the roots are contained, digging the hole—you need to anticipate and respond to questions at each step: How big should the hole be? How deep? Why? How is the root ball set in? During your drafting, you might even ask which of the steps need illustrations or photos to complete the teaching or, in other words, to fulfill your purpose for your audience.

When you're composing a text that is less concrete—an interpretation or analysis, perhaps—you might find that questioning helps you get from a rough outline to full paragraphs. One student was assigned to write an interpretation of song lyrics or a poem of his choice. The assignment also included a requirement that students illustrate some part of the song or poem. The student chose the song "Pumped Up Kicks" by Foster the People, listened to the song and read through the lyrics numerous times, brainstormed some ideas that focused on the song's main character, and wrote a rough outline.

ROUGH OUTLINE

Interpretation of "Pumped Up Kicks"

Main idea: If the song is Robert's "story," is there any way he, who shoots and murders peers, can be seen as a sympathetic character? Close, but no.

- Robert is alone and lonely, and that's something the audience can understand and maybe relate to.
- Robert has a negative relationship with the "other" kids, and the audience can understand that fact as a powerful motivator.

- Robert makes devastating choices, so extreme that it's hard for the audience to relate.

The student was comfortable enough with his main idea and proceeded to draft an introduction focusing on what makes a character sympathetic. The following shows how he went about developing a paragraph from the first point in his rough outline.

Point in the rough outline	The composer's questions	Draft paragraph
Robert is alone and lonely, and that's something the audience can understand and maybe relate to.	*How can I tell Robert is alone? Where do I see this in the lyrics? Does alone = lonely?*	The lyrics show us a boy, a "kid," whose "Daddy works a long day" and who spends the day unsupervised. Robert is alone in his house and alone in his thoughts as he spends idle time digging in "his dad's closet" and trying his father's cigarettes. There's not really a hint of any kind of relationship (at least a positive relationship) in the story.
	Do I care? Does his loneliness make him sympathetic?	The father comes "home late," probably repeatedly, and Robert is left waiting "for a long time." There doesn't seem to be a mother figure or siblings. Even if we can't relate to Robert, maybe we can understand his actions as being the result of an unloving home environment. His being alone and lonely generates sympathy.

As the student moves from outline to draft, he successfully identifies evidence from the lyrics to support his point. He still needs to consider images that might help him communicate his analysis of the lyrics. After all, his assignment asks him to illustrate a part of the poem or lyrics. He's off to a good start, however.

When you proceed from your ideas and notes to full sentences and strings of ideas, keep in mind that a *draft* is flexible. The goal is to get something down on paper that makes some sense and can be played with and questioned later by you, a peer, or another reader. It

helps to ask, anticipate, and respond to questions you have or your reader might have. And of course it helps to keep your purpose for writing and your audience in mind as you draft.

ACTIVITY MM11–1: Your understanding

To experiment with one type of organizing tool for a multimodal composition, try "reverse engineering" a brief video or a fairly simple Web site. Identify a video or Web site and strip it down to either an outline, a wireframe, or a storyboard.

ACTIVITY MM11–2: Your project

Take a current assignment and, as you work your way through your ideas for the assignment, try out at least one of the organizing tools discussed in this section. Write a brief reflective paragraph about whether the strategy was or was not helpful to you as you moved on to the drafting stage.

MM12 Emphasizing important information

When you look at a document, you'll notice that some information is emphasized, or treated more prominently, to catch the reader's attention or communicate a main idea. In print documents, emphasis is usually achieved by the placement of information on the page. Take a look at the sample documents, a résumé and a brochure, in Figures 12–1 and 12–2. What information jumps out at you? What information do you think is the most important in each one?

When you examine the résumé, think about the context and purpose of a résumé. The "work" a résumé does is to "sell" the author—to best portray his or her abilities, skills, and experiences. The author emphasizes his name with boldface type and centered placement. He presents categories that will be of interest to his reader in a consistent way. The second document, a brochure, would appear folded, with the panel on the right as the "cover." The emphasis is on a photograph of a puppy and a child. Why? The composer made choices to inspire the reader to act on behalf of the family pet.

Composers use different methods of emphasizing important information, depending on the type of composition they're producing. If you have written traditional essays, you may be used to creating emphasis with your words and sentence structure—using

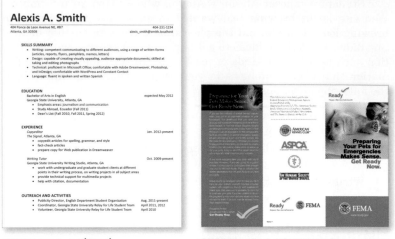

FIGURE 12–1 A RÉSUMÉ.   **FIGURE 12–2 A BROCHURE.** (*Source:* FEMA)

phrases like "and most important" or "the strongest evidence yet." In traditional essays, information is expressed in written words, and it's up to your readers to be able to discern what information is critical without the aid of visual cues. When you compose multimodal essays, you'll have to first determine what information is most important to emphasize, given your purpose and audience, and then how you can best emphasize that information, given your genre and modes.

MM12-a Determining what needs emphasis

Before you can make decisions about how to emphasize certain information, you need to decide what information is most crucial to convey. This decision depends on your audience and your purpose.

If your purpose is to inform and your audience is peers (other college students) who are new to the topic, you'll want to think about overarching categories of information and what might motivate your audience to engage with the information. If your purpose is to persuade your audience to embrace your position in a debate, the most important information to emphasize might be the evidence you provide to support your key points.

Student composer Alyson D'Amato, who created an informative Web site about brewing tea, wanted to emphasize the benefits of brewing loose leaf tea and the pleasures of creating custom blends. She didn't want these ideas to get buried under other basic information such as different kinds of tea leaves. To start identifying information that needs emphasis in your own composition, think about the following questions:

- What is your reason for composing? What are you trying to accomplish, and why?
- Who are your audience members? What information is going to be most appealing to them? Most convincing?
- What's the main thing you want your readers to remember after they've experienced your composition?

MM12-b Choosing a strategy for creating emphasis

In a text-only document with minimal design, the words themselves carry importance; that is, how you format words and sentences and where you place them help provide emphasis. You would probably express an important idea in a topic sentence at the start of a paragraph, for example, rather than bury it in the middle of a long paragraph. In a text-only document with design features, important ideas can be emphasized with font choice and by styling words with boldface, underline, italics, and type size. Look at the documents in Figure 12–3. From a glance, what would you assume to be the most important information in each one?

The large boldface text in the first and third examples is likely the most important information. The first example also includes a "pull quote," which draws readers' eyes to the right side of the page. The second example includes some boldface text and a bulleted list, which help key information stand out from the rest of the text. In the third example, readers might assume that the text block at the bottom of the page is less important than the spaced-out, right-aligned text at the top of the page.

Consider the front page of Alyson D'Amato's Web site (Figure 12–4). Perhaps the most important information on the front page is the list of links at the top of the page, which allows readers to see the different topics addressed on the Web site and to go to the different pages of the site. This navigation bar stays at the top of each page, so readers can easily move around on the site from whichever page they land on. D'Amato has also emphasized the photo of tea leaves—with her audience (tea novices) in mind.

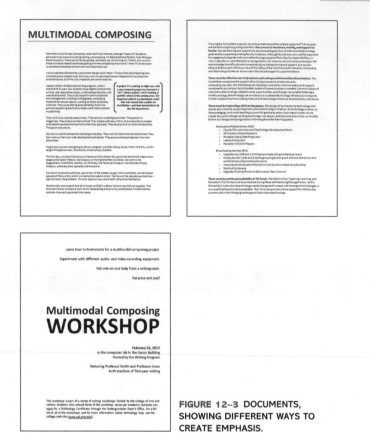

FIGURE 12-3 DOCUMENTS, SHOWING DIFFERENT WAYS TO CREATE EMPHASIS.

On the Web site home page, the body text appears in somewhat standard-size text, organized into paragraphs. The front page text is important, but perhaps not as important as the navigation bar.

If you listen to student composer Marisa Williamson's video, which argues that tragedies—even those experienced only on YouTube—knit us together, you'll notice that she repeats some audio clips throughout the video. This repetition of information makes it stand out as particularly important.

She repeats three key audio clips across her work:

- "The world is very different now." (John F. Kennedy)
- "Now is the time." (Martin Luther King Jr.)
- "We cannot turn back." (Martin Luther King Jr.)

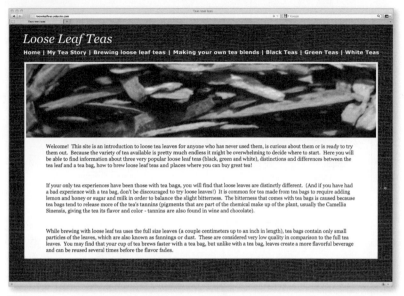

FIGURE 12-4 FIRST PAGE OF A WEB SITE, SHOWING LINKS, AN IMAGE, AND TEXT.

These clips contribute to her main idea that online video is now one of the primary ways that we experience formative events. She deliberately chose *not* to repeat a phrase that John F. Kennedy is perhaps most famous for: "Ask not what your country can do for you — ask what you can do for your country." Because this famous line is heard only once in Williamson's composition, it stands out as being particularly meaningful.

Another way that the student creates dramatic emphasis is by beginning and ending with audio clips of Ronald Reagan, US president in 1986 when the space shuttle *Challenger* disaster occurred.

You have a number of strategies for emphasizing important information at your disposal as you craft a multimodal piece. In a PowerPoint slide, you might style headings so that they communicate your key ideas prominently, and you might use bullet points to emphasize steps or points in your presentation. In an advertisement, you might add white space around a product shot to call attention to it. In a podcast, you might pause and use silence for emphasis. In a video, you might use subtitles to reinforce a message. Considering your purpose for composing, determining your audience, and understanding the genre in which you are composing are important steps in figuring out how to make an impact.

ACTIVITY MM12–1: Your understanding

In section MM8, you looked at the home pages of a few Web sites to identify the primary audience of each (see p. MM-59). Take a look again at the following sites, with emphasis in mind:

- the main Web site of your school
- the Web site of a professor at your school
- the Web site of a fast-food restaurant in your area
- the Web site of a small, locally owned restaurant in your area
- the Web site of the company that made the car you drive or that makes the car you'd like to drive
- the Web site for a branch or an agency of the US government (for example, the White House, the IRS, the FBI)
- the Web site for an individual who serves in the US government (such as a member of Congress)

As you look at each multimodal text, identify what information the composer seems to be emphasizing. How do you know it's important? What are some of the techniques used to highlight the most important information? Write brief notes for each piece, and be prepared to discuss them in class.

ACTIVITY MM12–2: Your project

For a project you are currently working on, make notes about the information you want to emphasize and some strategies you can use to do so. Take into consideration your purpose, your audience, and the genre you are working in. What textual formatting options might you use to draw attention to your key points? What visuals might you embed to support those points? Are there audio clips (dialogue, music, sound effects) or video clips that might help articulate the main points in your project?

MM13 Revising and editing your multimodal project

Very few writers sit down, write a first draft of a paper, and submit it for a successful grade. More typically, writers work on a draft in chunks, circling back occasionally to reread and rewrite. You may find that your instructors build time into an assignment for feedback, revising, and editing. Even if they don't, it's useful to set aside some time so that you can move comfortably from a first or second draft

to a final piece. Revising and editing a multimodal composition may take substantially more time than revising and editing a traditional essay.

Your handbook includes advice about revising and editing. For the purposes of this brief discussion, keep in mind the following distinctions:

In general, **revising** involves

- rethinking your point or purpose
- reshaping your approach to fit your audience's needs
- reorganizing or strengthening evidence to help you achieve your purpose
- rearranging whole parts of your composition
- revisiting your message

In general, **editing** involves

- checking to see if sentences and paragraphs progress logically
- adding transitions where necessary to improve coherence
- changing wordy phrases
- deleting sentences that are off-topic
- making sure that word choice is precise and tailored to the purpose and audience

When revising and editing a traditional, words-only document, a writer might move around, add, or delete whole passages or sentences in a word processing program. The writer might print out a draft to mark corrections, changes, or points that need more clarification. The processes of revising a multimodal project, however, might be quite different, depending on the modes used. The overall point of revising and editing, whether your composition is multimodal or monomodal, is to make your work stronger, clearer, better organized, and on target for your purpose and audience.

MM13-a Seeking and using feedback

Before you revise and edit, it may help to seek feedback from classmates, your instructor, a tutor, or a friend. Tell each reviewer whether you want feedback about larger, more global issues (organization, main point, use of audio/visual/textual evidence, overall message) or surface-level issues (clear sentences, precise words, sentence logic). In other words, tell reviewers whether you are approaching a revising

stage or an editing stage. Before you share a draft with a reviewer, think about three key questions you might want your reviewer to answer, and share those questions with him or her.

After student composer Alyson D'Amato had made initial decisions based on her purpose, audience, and content and after she had outlined and drafted her project, an informative Web site about tea, she met with a tutor at her school's writing center to get feedback on her site. Figure 13–1 shows a page from her draft site. She asked the tutor the following questions:

1. The assignment says that we have to have a good navigation, or a clear introduction and way for the reader/viewer to move through the composition. Is the navigation clear? How can I improve it?

2. I'm not sure about the pictures I've included, but I don't know what I would replace them with. Can you comment on the visuals?

3. Do you think that the text is well written and flows well? Can you point out areas that could be stronger?

D'Amato and her tutor spent some time looking at her site, and the tutor had D'Amato read parts of it out loud. They also looked at

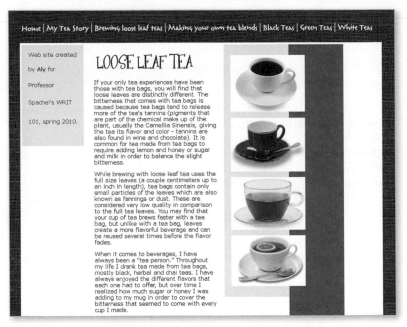

FIGURE 13–1 DRAFT STUDENT PROJECT: AN INFORMATIVE WEB SITE.

a few other informative Web sites for ideas and inspiration. D'Amato left with a set of priorities for revising her work. The following are her revision goals.

ALYSON D'AMATO'S REVISION GOALS

- There's too much to read on each page. Streamline. We looked at another Web site with similar navigation but more manageable content. We came up with a way to break up the text.

- The tea photos are cool, but they don't really make sense, especially since one has a tea bag in it and my site is about brewing loose leaf teas. Maybe replace with images of loose leaf tea.

- The tutor also asked why I chose the font for "LOOSE LEAF TEA," and I just thought it looked cool. We looked at some other tea sites, and they all used a more elegant type of font that might be easier to read and more appealing to people interested in tea. Choose new font.

- The site will need more of an introduction—the tutor said I just jumped right into it here. There are also chunks of info that don't really fit or flow well. I marked those and need to revise them. NOTE TO SELF!!! Do this before reworking the text on different pages!

- The tutor also asked why I took up so much room on the left side with my name and class info. He suggested that because my audience is potential tea fans generally, I might want to cut the class-specific info, because it really makes this look like a student project, which some people might not take seriously.

Creating a list of goals is a good way to make the transition between feedback and revising. Keep in mind that you don't have to make every change a reviewer suggests. Look at the reviewer's suggestions through the lens of your own purpose, audience, and assignment. Not every suggestion is going to be right for your project. If you seek feedback from three reviewers, however, and all three say that your project seems a little hard to follow, you know that organization is going to be one area in which you'll want to focus your revision efforts.

MM13-b Revising and remixing a multimodal composition

Writers typically revise a draft by moving sentences or paragraphs around their paper. Word processing software makes it easy for writers to cut and paste chunks of text in a words-only draft. When a writer, for example, reads the final paragraph in a draft and

realizes—either on his or her own or with a reader's help—that the main point is buried in the concluding paragraph, it's easy enough to move a sentence or group of sentences from one place to another and rewrite as needed.

When revising a multimodal piece, you might have to ask different kinds of revision questions depending on the mode(s) you've chosen to communicate your main idea.

- In revising a speech, you might ask, *Where is it important to pause and perhaps seek audience interaction? How can my speech be stronger with the use of props or visual aids?*

- In revising a slide show presentation, you might ask, *Is the balance of text and visuals right? Do I need this whole table as evidence, or can I use just a detail from it? Are the slides progressing at the right pace for my audience, mainly senior citizens?*

- In revising a video, you might ask, *Would narration help to provide "glue" between the testimony of my interviewees? Is the background music too distracting?*

Thinking about revision as *remix* can be helpful in approaching a multimodal project. *Remix* is a term typically used to describe the process of taking an original audio track and adding other elements. Perhaps one of the most infamous remixes in recent times was Danger Mouse's 2004 release of *The Grey Album*. To produce the album, Danger Mouse took Jay-Z's *Black Album* (2003) and remixed it with the Beatles' *White Album* (1968). Together, the lyrics and music from both albums—mixed and merged together—took on an entirely different tone and meaning.

A useful way to think about revision with a multimodal composition is that you are "remixing" your own work—taking an original piece or set of pieces and rearranging them, resequencing them, and perhaps adding elements. This remixing might result in a composition with more impact, better focus, or more awareness of the audience.

Student composer Marisa Williamson found that to revise her video essay, she had to keep circling back and remixing the elements of her draft. She had a lot of what she needed in her first draft; for her, revising meant rearranging in response to feedback from her classmates.

For example, when Williamson initially drafted her video piece, she sequenced the images and video chronologically—she included the images and video of John F. Kennedy's assassination first (1963), followed by footage related to Martin Luther King Jr.'s assassination (1968) and the space shuttle *Challenger* disaster (1986), and ended with video of the September 11 terrorist attacks in New York City (2001).

Fellow students who saw the draft suggested that she didn't need to tell the story chronologically to make her point. She resequenced the clips and even tried looping, or repeating, some of the clips for emphasis. Also, Williamson wasn't sure how she wanted to include her own words in her video. In her first draft, she included her words by scrolling them along the bottom of the movie. Her classmates, however, suggested that this was distracting and that it might be interesting to record and layer her own voice over the music. She tried that at the revising stage.

MM13-c Editing a multimodal composition

Editing is a stage in which a composer takes a closer look at the composition and asks, *Is it clear? Does it make sense?* Editing a words-only composition means looking at words and sentences and the transitions between sentences and paragraphs. Editing a multimodal composition can be a bit more complicated, in part because multimodal projects require composers to work across different modes and sometimes across different software. As you edit your project, you might find the questions in the following chart helpful.

Editing multimodal compositions

Editing words

- Have you chosen the clearest, most appropriate words for your purpose and audience?
- Are your sentences and paragraphs in logical order?
- Have you included transitions between sentences and paragraphs to improve the flow of your ideas?
- Could your ideas be expressed in more concise language?
- Do grammar or spelling errors distract from your message?

Editing sounds

- Is the volume appropriate? Do any sounds drown out other elements?
- Is the pace of the narration right? Not too slow or too fast?
- Do you need more sound or more silence?
- Is your sound synched properly to any static or moving images that go with it?

Editing static images

- Have you chosen the clearest, most appropriate images for your purpose and audience?
- Do you need more visual evidence? Do you have the right kind of visuals? Would a graph, for example, be better than a photograph for your composition?
- Have you used captions as needed for the images? Some visuals can't speak for themselves.
- Are the images you've chosen presented at an appropriate size?

Editing moving images

- If you're using video clips, is the length appropriate?
- Is the purpose of the moving images clear in your composition?
- Are the moving images emphasizing the right content?

Editing for consistency and clarity

- If you've made changes in one mode (edited words in the narration, for instance), do you need to make changes in another (edit words that appear on-screen)?
- If you've produced slides, do they have a consistent design?
- Are you using colors, font sizes, and headings purposefully and consistently?
- If you have navigation elements in your project, is it clear to your users/viewers how to get from one place to another?

Crediting and citing

- Have you cited the works you're quoting from, paraphrasing, or summarizing?
- Have you credited the artists whose music you've used?
- Have you credited the creators or photographers of the images you've used?
- Have you credited the composers of the video clips you've used?

ACTIVITY MM13-1: Your understanding

Popular examples of remixes are multimodal compositions in which composers rearrange the events in movie trailers to create a different, alternative tone or meaning. If you search the Web for "remixed" or "recut" movie trailers, you may find one that positions *The Hunger Games* as a comedy and *Twilight* as a creepy stalker film. Find two or three different remixed movie trailers. Identify what elements are probably "original" to the trailer, and

then identify what elements have been remixed, added, or changed. What effect does the remix have? Why?

ACTIVITY MM13–2: Your project

Think about a project you're currently working on. Make a plan to seek feedback from a teacher, tutor, classmate, or friend. Make a list of three or four questions you want to ask this person. What sort of advice or feedback do you hope to get? After you meet with this person, compose a brief list of revision goals.

≡ MM14 Integrating and documenting sources

Most composers at some point depend on source material—words, data, audio, or images that come from elsewhere. Writers in medicine depend on clinical studies; caseworkers in the social sciences depend on interviews; filmmakers depend on scripts. Responsible composers integrate and document their sources according to the conventions of their field. These conventions don't always translate well from field to field. Imagine watching a movie and having citations to reference material appear on the screen throughout the movie. Likewise, imagine reading an academic article that makes claims but offers no support and no citations. When you are composing, you will want to pay attention to the expectations for crediting your sources in the type of composition you are creating.

MM14-a Understanding why documenting sources is important

Giving formal credit to sources is necessary for a few key reasons. Documenting sources allows you to

- make evident to an audience that you have done your homework, researched the topic thoroughly, and are aware of larger conversations, discussions, and research related to the topic
- direct an audience to the original material that you gathered and used to conduct research and write up your findings
- give credit where credit is due, acknowledging your use of someone else's ideas—whether they're expressed in written words, static or moving images, sound, or multiple modes.

You may be familiar with instructors' expectations about different documentation styles (MLA, APA, *Chicago*, CSE). Your handbook covers how to cite sources in your written work using one of these styles.

MM14-b Knowing when a citation is needed

Sources don't always have to be formal academic articles or books. One of the trickiest aspects of citing your sources and documenting your work is recognizing what should be cited, regardless of the type of composition you are crafting.

You should generally cite a source in these cases:

- when you use or refer to somebody else's words or ideas from a magazine, book, newspaper, song, TV program, movie, Web page, computer program, letter, advertisement, or any other medium
- when you use information obtained through interviewing another person
- when you use data from experiments that you did not conduct
- when you use diagrams, illustrations, charts, or photos that you did not create
- when you use audio or video clips that you did not create

Typically, you do not need to document a source in these cases:

- when you are writing from your own experiences, your own observations, your own insights, your own thoughts, or your own conclusions about a subject
- when you are using "common knowledge"—folklore, common-sense observations, or shared information within your field of study or cultural group
- when you are compiling generally accepted facts
- when you are writing up your own experimental result

MM14-c Determining how to integrate sources in a multimodal composition

The Internet makes it easy to find images, photographs, articles, songs, sounds, and other material with a few clicks. With a fast Internet connection, downloading such materials is convenient. Most computer programs, from spreadsheet applications to presentation software to word processing tools, allow users to include images, sounds, and the like in their documents. Video production applications allow composers to include audio tracks and text on-screen.

Much of what you find on the Web, however, is owned by others—in other words, it is the copyright-protected property of other individuals. This doesn't mean that students can't use the materials for class projects, but being a college writer means knowing how to integrate and acknowledge sources responsibly and correctly.

When you integrate words (a quotation from, a paraphrase of, or a summary of source material) into a words-only document, you will typically do so with a signal phrase and a parenthetical reference.

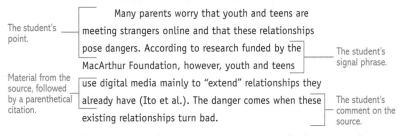

The student's point.

Many parents worry that youth and teens are meeting strangers online and that these relationships pose dangers. According to research funded by the MacArthur Foundation, however, youth and teens

The student's signal phrase.

Material from the source, followed by a parenthetical citation.

use digital media mainly to "extend" relationships they already have (Ito et al.). The danger comes when these existing relationships turn bad.

The student's comment on the source.

In multimodal projects, however, using a signal phrase and a parenthetical reference may be disruptive. Slide show composers who include images on slides usually do so with design in mind, placing images near key words or ideas for emphasis. During a talk, the presenter might refer to a particular image: *As you can see from this table, the number of people in America who identify themselves as biracial has tripled in the past fifteen years.* The speaker may give the source of the information in the talk, include a source line in smaller type under the image, or include a bibliography in a final slide.

You may have a great deal of flexibility when *integrating* sources in a multimodal project. College instructors will expect you to *document* your sources; in doing so, you will have a little less flexibility. Be sure to ask your instructor for guidelines.

MM14-d Figuring out how to document sources in a multimodal composition

Composers can cite sources in different ways, for different modes. Student Marisa Williamson provides a separate works cited page for her video essay "To the Children of America," because that is what the assignment requires. She credits the owners of the music she used, the audio clips she used, and the images and video she used. Her works cited list provides enough information for her audience to find the complete, original files that she edited for her project. If she creates a video essay for another course, she might follow a convention typical of movies and include a credits section at the end of her video.

Another example of how sources are cited differently in different types of compositions is shown on the works cited page of Alyson D'Amato's Web site. D'Amato was, for much of the content, the expert. That is, she didn't need to do a lot of research because she knew a great deal about selecting and brewing tea. She was interested in learning more about tea rituals and tea history, so she cited the works she consulted as she worked on her site, and she also created a list of links to Web sites she mentioned on her own site (see Figure 14–1).

Identifying what citation conventions are typical of the delivery mode you plan to use and following those conventions is part of multimodal composing. See the chart on pages MM-98 and MM-99.

The list of genres in the chart is not exhaustive, but it gives some sense of the ways in which composers of multimodal works can document the use of materials and information they did not create. Depending on the course for which you are composing, you may be asked to consult a particular academic citation style, such as MLA, APA, or *Chicago*. See your handbook for more on documenting sources in these styles.

Works Cited and Links

Home | My Tea Story | Brewing loose leaf teas | Making your own tea blends | Black Teas | Green Teas | White Teas

Works Cited

Elliott, Stuart. "It's in the Bag—the Tea Bag, That Is." *New York Times.* New York Times, 13 Oct. 2008. Web. 5 Oct. 2009. <http://www.nytimes.com/2008/10/13/business/media/13adnewsletter1.html?ref=tea>.

"How to Brew Green Tea: The Top Ten Reasons Your Tea Didn't Turn Out Stellar." *O-Cha.com.* O-Cha.com Japanese Green Tea & Matcha, 2009. Web. 3 Oct. 2009. <http://www.o-cha.com/brewing-green-tea.html>.

"How to Brew Loose Leaf Tea." *Arbor Teas.* Arbor Teas, 2009. Web. 5 Oct. 2009. <http://www.arborteas.com/pages/brew-loose-tea.html>.

Jeanroy, Amy. "Make Your Own Herb Tea Blend." *About.com.* About.com, n.d. Web. 3 Oct. 2009. <http://herbgardens.about.com/od/herbrecipes/a/HerbTeas.htm>.

Kondo, Dorinne. "The Way of Tea: A Symbolic Analysis." *Man* 20.2 (1985): 287–306. *JStor.* Web. 5 Oct. 2009.

"Make Your Own Tea." *Farmers' Almanac.* Almanac Publishing, 1 Sept. 2007. Web. 3 Oct. 2009. <http://www.farmersalmanac.com/food/2007/09/01/make-your-own-tea/>.

Marshall, Eliot. "How Natural Is the Science of Brewing?" *Science.* AAAS, 23 Feb. 1979. Web. 5 Oct. 2009. <http://www.sciencemag.org/content/203/4382/731.full.pdf>.

"Mini Tea Chest." *Sundial Gardens Tea Chest.* Sundial Gardens, n.d. Web. 5 Oct. 2009. <http://www.sundialgardens.com/miniTeaChestinfo.htm>.

"The Strength of Tea." *British Medical Journal* 2.1405 (1887): 1229. *JStor.* Web. 5 Oct. 2009.

"Tea." *New York Times.* New York Times, 2009. Web. 5 Oct. 2009. <http://topics.nytimes.com/top/reference/timestopics/subjects/t/tea/index.html>.

Internet Tea Vendors

Empire Tea and Coffee
Imperialtea.com
Teavana.com
Silkroadstea.com
Specialteas.com
Sundialgardens.com

FIGURE 14–1 WEB PAGE SHOWING WORKS CITED, INCLUDING LINKS TO RELATED WEB SITES.

Documentation conventions for different genres

Genre	Documentation convention	Reason
Essay, article, or scientific report	Typically in a works cited or reference list at the end of the essay	For an author to show that she or he has done research and thoroughly explored the topic For others to access this original work that the author consulted
Slide show presentation	At the very end, embedded in a separate slide typically called "sources" or "works cited"	For an author to show that she or he has done research and thoroughly explored the topic For others to access this original work that the author consulted To give credit and provide information for video clips, music, and other material produced by someone other than the presentation's composer
Song lyrics	Usually in the liner notes, where the artist gives formal credit or points toward permission to use copyrighted lyrics	To give credit to the original author of the lyrics or text being set to music
Music	Usually in the liner notes, where the artist gives formal credit or points toward permission to use copyrighted music	To give credit to the original artist or composer

Genre	Documentation convention	Reason
Full-length movie	At the very end, embedded within what are typically called the "closing credits"	To list cast and crew To provide location information and acknowledge the help of a community To include complete names and artists for songs used in the movie For major motion pictures, there are strict standards regarding who gets credited and in what order.
Short video	At the very end, embedded within what are typically called the "credits"	For an author to show that she or he has done research and thoroughly explored the topic For others to access this original work that the author consulted To give credit and provide information for video clips, music, and other material produced by someone other than the video's composer
News broadcast	Usually mentioned by the reporter orally within the story itself Can be a mention of a story from another news source Can be credit given to an ordinary citizen	For the station or reporter to give credit to the original person who broke the story or provided the information To include more perspectives and viewpoints in a story

ACTIVITY MM14–1: Your understanding

Review a writing assignment you recently completed that required you to produce an essay or some other traditional document. How did you integrate and document your sources for the assignment? Imagine re-creating the composition in another format—perhaps as a video or a slide show presentation. How would your handling of the sources change?

ACTIVITY MM14–2: Your project

It's important to keep a working bibliography whenever you work with sources. Consult your handbook's guidelines for compiling and maintaining a working bibliography, and create a working bibliography for your current project.

MM15 Presenting or publishing your project

When you produce a typical essay, you usually turn in a printed, paper copy of that essay to your instructor, or perhaps you turn it in by uploading the word-processed document to a course management system like Blackboard or CompClass. Submitting the work is easy because most students have access to printers and because most essays—even those with a few images—are small electronic files.

Files that include multimodal projects, however, can be extremely large. Or you may have produced a multi*file* project. Submitting and sharing the project sometimes cannot be done by e-mail or on paper.

It's important to consider where and how you will publish your multimodal project. Will you post a video on a video-sharing site like YouTube? Will you create a Web site that your school can host? Will you upload a slide show to your course page? Your instructor may give guidelines about sharing your work with your intended audience. This section includes some tips for thinking through this final stage of the project.

MM15-a Knowing your options for presenting and publishing multimodal works

The first step in deciding how to present or publish your project is knowing the different spaces available to you.

Your instructor may recommend specific presentation or publication spaces for your project. For instance, some schools have their own intranet where students can store projects. Your instructor may prefer that you upload your work to a course management site or system.

There are many other options to consider. You may need to poke around online or consult with peers about the following:

Video-hosting sites: Web sites that allow you to upload video and that will generate a stable URL for your video. (One example: YouTube)

Web-creation sites: Web sites where you can compile and create your own Web site. These often allow you to copy and paste text, add images, and create links. (One example: Weebly)

Web-hosting sites: Web sites where you can upload your Web files and create your own Web site with a unique URL. These sites often have built-in Web-creation options, too. (One example: GoDaddy)

Slide show creation and hosting sites: Web sites that allow you to build a slide show presentation and store it for others to view. (One example: Prezi)

MM15-b Considering the pros and cons of the spaces available for presenting and publishing multimodal work

If you have a choice about how and where to share your work, you may want to consider the pros and cons of different spaces. See the chart on pages MM-102 and MM-103.

Once you've chosen a specific type of space for creating or hosting your project and then chosen a specific site, you'll need to familiarize yourself with the options that site provides. Your instructor may be able to help. You will probably need answers to at least a few of the following questions:

- Do you need an account to work in the space? If so, do you have to pay for the account?
- Will your readers/viewers need a password to access your work?
- Will your readers/viewers have to set up an account to access your work?
- Will your readers/viewers have to download or install any special software to view your work?
- How long will your work be available on the site?
- Will ads appear in or near your work when it is on the site?

Presentation spaces for multimodal projects

Presentation space	Pros	Cons
Your campus course management space	Password-protected, so only your instructor and perhaps other students in your class can access your work	Typically does not offer building and creation tools—just offers storage space Usually limited in terms of file size for student projects (so a 10 MB slide show might be fine, but a 100 MB video project might be too big)
Video-hosting sites	Allow you to upload and store big files Allow you to create videos that aren't software dependent (i.e., users/viewers don't have to have a specific type of software to see the video) Usually allow users to post comments and share feedback	Are often advertisement-based, so ads may appear around or even on top of your video Sometimes generate long and hard-to-remember URLs
Web-creation sites	Can make Web site creation and design easy	Are sometimes subscription- or fee-based (you have to pay to use them) Some are less intuitive than others
Web-hosting sites	Allow you to purchase your own URL Usually provide storage space for many different file types and sizes	Are sometimes subscription- or fee-based (you have to pay to use them) Can have complicated interfaces, making uploading your content difficult

Presentation space	Pros	Cons
Slide show creation and hosting sites	Allow you to create slide show presentations that aren't software dependent (i.e., users/viewers don't have to have a specific type of software to see the presentation) Can make slide show creation and design easy	Are sometimes subscription- or fee-based (you have to pay to use them) Some are less intuitive than others

MM15-c Making your project accessible and usable

In earlier sections, you read about taking into consideration the needs of your audience. Often you need to think about whether your project will be accessible and usable to your audience. If it's not, you won't be able to communicate your message. *Accessibility* typically refers to someone's physical ability to access something. For instance, a building that has only steps at its entry is not physically accessible for people using wheelchairs. In terms of multimodal projects, accessibility refers to someone's ability to hear, see, or generally put to use a text. Multimodal texts that are not accessible have a more limited audience. For example, a person with hearing deficits might be unable to use a video lecture online because she can't hear the speaker and no transcript is provided.

Usability typically refers to ease of use — how easy it is to navigate a Web site or learn to use a product, for example. In terms of multimodal projects, usability has to do with how easy or difficult it is for the audience to find, experience, and understand the composer's ideas. For example, if a multimodal text needs to be downloaded for viewing, the composer can improve usability by reducing the file size to accommodate slower Internet connections.

Not everyone has a fast Internet connection or access to a computer. Not all of the audience for your multimodal work can see or hear, or can see or hear well. You can't plan for every possible audience need, but you can compose multimodal pieces that allow you to reach the widest possible audience. Here are some guidelines to keep in mind.

Consider what format works best for your audience. For many projects, your instructor is your main audience. If your instructor doesn't tell you the format in which you should submit your project, ask. It's better to know up front than to wrestle later with converting a complete project from one interface or delivery system to another. For other projects, you might have different audiences—the campus community, for instance, or YouTube users in general. To best create for your audience, you have to know their technical expectations and also the technical specifications of your delivery choice. For instance, if your instructor has asked you to upload your project to your course management system, that system might have a maximum upload file size, so you'll have to compress your file in order to share it. YouTube and other video-sharing spaces often have time restrictions; YouTube restricts general users to ten-minute clips.

Build in accessibility features. If, for instance, you suspect that your audience might include people who don't hear well or at all, you might add captions to your project. The captions might describe the sounds in your video ([MUSIC] or [LOUD FOOTSTEPS]) and might also offer written text for what's being heard or said in your piece. If you suspect that your audience might include people with vision difficulties, you might provide a text-only transcript of your piece. Most people with visual impairment use a program called a "screen reader," a kind of software that reads text to them. Screen readers, however, cannot easily translate text saved in a slide show presentation or in a movie. Including a transcript of your piece for a screen reader helps make your work accessible to those with vision problems. Providing captions and transcripts can also help reach members of your audience who experience technical difficulties and cannot get clear audio or a clear visual display.

ACTIVITY MM15–1: Your understanding

Find one additional example site for each of the types included in the list in MM15-a. Once you've chosen your example sites, read through their "about" pages and also look through the help areas of their sites. Think about your own degree of technical expertise and your experience with each kind of site. How easily could you become proficient in using each site?

ACTIVITY MM15–2: Your project

For a project you're currently planning or drafting, write a brief page of notes about what you may need to consider so that your audience will find your composition usable and accessible.

Acknowledgments

Figure 1–1: Grecian urn. Illustration by John Keats from Public Domain.

Figure 1–2: Geoglyph photograph. Courtesy of the U.S. National Park Service/U.S. Department of the Interior. Petroglyph photograph. Copyright © Pgiam/istockphoto.com.

Figure 1–3: Illuminated manuscript. Copyright © Duncan Walker/ istockphoto.com.

Figure 1–4: Quick Response Code. QR Code is a registered trademark of DENSO WAVE Incorporated. http://www.qrcode.com/faqpatent-e.html.

Figure 1–5: Numbered math equations. Courtesy of http://umsolver.com. "UMS software's free Algebraic Equation Solver will solve and explain any algebraic equation or system of equations."

Figure 1–6: Tectonic plates. Illustration courtesy of the U.S. Geological Survey. Simkin and others, 2006.

Figure 1–7: Music collage. Copyright © Gilbert Mayer/Superstock.

Figure 1–8: "Where is your family?" billlboard image. Copyright © Sonda Dawes/The Image Works.

Figure 2–1c: Pets brochure. Courtesy of FEMA/www.ready.gov.

Page MM-28: River photograph. Copyright © straga/shutterstock.com.

Page MM-28: Sketch of bridge. Copyright © Danussa/shutterstock.com.

Page MM-28: Map of Michigan. Copyright © Jami Garrison/istockphoto.com.

Page MM-28: River clip art. Copyright © Sapik/shutterstock.com.

Page MM-29: Flood tracking bar graph. Illustration courtesy of the U.S. Geological Survey.

Page MM-29: Elwha River diagram. Illustration courtesy of the U.S. Geological Survey. Duda, J. J., Warrick, J. A., and Magirl, C. S., 2011, Elwha River dam removal—Rebirth of a river: U.S. Geological Survey Fact Sheet 2011-3097, 4 p. Illustrator: Jonathan A. Warrick.

Figure 4–1: Woman washing hair illustration. Copyright © RetroClipArt/ shutterstock.com.

Page MM-31: German shepherd photograph. Copyright © gualtiero boffi/ shutterstock.com.

Figure 4–2: Dandelion photograph. Copyright © Dleonis/Dreamstime.com.

Figure 4–3: Migrant Mother by Dorothea Lange, 1936. Library of Congress/ Farm Security Administration, Office of War Information Photograph.

Page MM-34: CNN frame grab of Saddam Hussein statue falling. Uniphotos/ Newscom. Saddam Hussein statue toppling photograph. Copyright © Robert Nickelsberg/Getty Images.

Page MM-35: Obama HOPE poster. Courtesy of SHEPARD FAIREY/ OBEYGIANT.COM.

Page MM-35: POPE illustration. Courtesy of © Michael Ian Weinfeld.

Page MM-35: CHANGE INTO A TRUCK poster. Copyright © Timothy P. Doyle, 2009, www.mrdoyle.com.

Page MM-35: VERY GRADUAL CHANGE poster. Copyright © Mike Rosulek, 2009.

Figure 5–1: Illustration with photographs, by Eadweard Muybridge, 1878, Courtesy of the Library of Congress Prints and Photographs Division Washington, D.C. 20540 USA.

Figure 5–2: Flip still from *Cloverfield*. Moviestore Collection Ltd./Alamy.

Page MM-42: "Fried egg"/"brain on drugs" PSA image. The Partnership for a Drug-Free America, Inc.

Page MM-43: "Touch the Rainbow" Skittles advertisement. Images used with permission from Wm. Wrigley Jr. Company. Copyright © 2011. All rights reserved. SKITTLES, the S Device, and all affiliated designs are trademarks of Wm. Wrigley Jr. Company or its affiliates. Title: Touch Skittles on YouTube; Client: Wrigley Canada; Product/Service: Skittles; Agency: BBDO Toronto; Writer: Chris Joakim; Art Director: Mike Donaghey; Creative Directors: Carlos Moreno, Peter Ignazi; Account Management: Chitty Krishnappa, Bhreagh Rathbun; Producer: Ann Caverly; Planner: Zach Klein; Marketing Management: Dan Alvo, Laura Amantea, Thomas Tse; Directors: Woods & Low; Production house: OPC/FamilyStyle; Executive Producers: Harland Weiss, Donovan Boden; Producer: Dwight Phipps; Director of Photography: Vinit Borrison; Editorial: Griff Henderson, Posterboy Edit; Visual FX: AXYZ; Color Transfer: Notch; Audio: Eggplant; Online producer: Amy Miranda—Lunch; Online programming/FX: Pixel Pushers; Media: OMD; Seeding: Denizen.

Page MM-43: Man eating Skittles advertisement. Images used with permission from Wm. Wrigley Jr. Company. Copyright © 2011. All rights reserved. SKITTLES, the S Device, and all affiliated designs are trademarks of Wm. Wrigley Jr. Company or its affiliates. Title: Touch Skittles on YouTube; Client: Wrigley Canada; Product/Service: Skittles; Agency: BBDO Toronto; Writer: Chris Joakim; Art Director: Mike Donaghey; Creative Directors: Carlos Moreno, Peter Ignazi; Account Management: Chitty Krishnappa, Bhreagh Rathbun; Producer: Ann Caverly; Planner: Zach Klein; Marketing Management: Dan Alvo, Laura Amantea, Thomas Tse; Directors: Woods & Low; Production house: OPC/FamilyStyle; Executive Producers: Harland Weiss, Donovan Boden; Producer: Dwight Phipps; Director of Photography: Vinit Borrison; Editorial: Griff Henderson, Posterboy Edit; Visual FX: AXYZ; Color Transfer: Notch; Audio: Eggplant; Online producer: Amy Miranda—Lunch; Online programming/FX: Pixel Pushers; Media: OMD; Seeding: Denizen.

Figure 6–1: Cheetah PSA advertisement. Used with permission © World Wildlife Fund/wwf.org.

Page MM-50: Dragon Age II video game inventory screen. Dragon Age II image used with permission of Electronic Arts Inc.

Alyson D'Amato, "Loose Leaf Teas" Web site. Used with permission.

King Anyi Howell podcast. This story was produced by Youth Radio, a Peabody Award–winning media production company.

Marisa Williamson, "To the Children of America" video essay. Used with permission.

Index

Manufactured in the United States of America.

7   6   5   4   3   2
f   e   d   c   b   a

For information, write: Bedford/St. Martin's, 75 Arlington Street, Boston, MA 02116   (617-399-4000)

ISBN 978-1-4576-1779-9

ACKNOWLEDGMENTS

Acknowledgments and copyrights can be found at the back of the book on pages MM-105 to MM-106, which constitute an extension of the copyright page. It is a violation of the law to reproduce these selections by any means whatsoever without the written permission of the copyright holder.

MM

Understanding and Composing Multimodal Projects

A Hacker Handbooks Supplement

Dànielle Nicole DeVoss
Michigan State University

BEDFORD / ST. MARTIN'S   BOSTON ◆ NEW YORK